LEADERSHIP FOR LEADERS

Michael Williams

Thorogood Publishing Limited
10-12 Rivington Street
London EC2A 3DU

Telephone: 020 7749 4748
Fax: 020 7729 6110
Email: info@thorogood.ws
Web: www.thorogood.ws

Books Network International Inc
3 Front Street, Suite 331
Rollinsford, NH 30869, USA

Telephone: +603 749 9171
Fax: +603 749 6155
Email: bizbks@aol.com

A CIP catalogue record for this book is
available from the British Library.

PB: ISBN 1 85418 350 8
HB: ISBN 1 85418 355 9

Cover and book designed in the UK by Driftdesign.

Printed in India by Replika Press.

Dedication

For Brenda
For her love and caring, over our many years together

The author

Michael Williams M.Sc. is an international management consultant who established his company, Michael Williams & Partners in 1979 and now works closely with associate companies in Geneva, Vienna and Copenhagen. He is also a director on the Board of British Ceramic Tile, based in Devon, in the UK.

His main clients include leading Business Schools, e.g. IMD at Lausanne and the Theseus Institute, located in Nice, as well as several universities and a wide range of companies and consultancies throughout Europe, Canada and the United States.

He is the author, or co-author, of many books in the fields of leadership, management practice and organizational psychology, including:

- *Mastering Leadership*
- *Enabling – Beyond Empowering*
- *Test your Management Skills*
- *The War for Talent*

His areas of specialization include senior executive development, the identification of leadership potential, transforming corporate culture and team development, using several unique and exclusive methods.

He draws on over twenty years' managerial experience in the printing, iron and steel, engineering, automotive and ceramic industries, including roles in manufacturing, sales and marketing, HR and organization development.

Mike is a member of the British Psychological Society, the Institute of Directors and the Association of Management Education & Development.

He originally read psychology, with moral philosophy and subsequently took his M.Sc., by research, at The University of Aston, in the fields of influencing management performance and the identification of executive potential.

He served full-time – and subsequently as a volunteer reservist – in the Royal Navy (Intelligence) and the Royal Marines (SBS and Commando). His various roles included – Russian linguist, frogman-canoeist, commando rifle-troop officer and second-in-command of a combined SBS-Commando RMR unit. He draws considerably on these experiences in his approach to leadership development and management training in the business world.

Acknowledgements

A great many people, among them some outstanding leaders, have provided opportunities for me to pursue my study of leadership in management and have contributed so much to the thinking that lies behind this book. To them, I owe an enormous debt of gratitude.

Especially helpful and always so positive in their contributions – as well as a challenge and fun to work with – are the following clients, several of whom I have worked with for a good many years. Their knowledge and skills remain invaluable in my own development and they include:

- Howard Mann, OBE, formerly President and CEO, McCain Foods, Toronto
- John Bridgeman, formerly Director General of the Office of Fair Trading
- Dr. Patrick Haren, Group CEO, Viridian
- Harry McCracken, CEO, Northern Ireland Electricity
- Jean-Francois Diet, Director General, Europ Assistance, Vienna
- Dr. Chiara Bolognesi, Co-ordinator, Management Development, Generali, Mogliano Veneto
- Dr Jan Hein van Joolen, VP, Group Leadership Development, ABN Amro Bank, Amsterdam
- Dr. Ole Staib-Jensen, President, MbO, Copenhagen
- David Brown, Senior Director, Global Learning Center, Organon, Oss, The Netherlands
- Dr Hein Aelbers, Regional Director, Organon, Budapest
- George Telfer, The Leadership Trust

- Mirjam Niessen, Programme Co-ordinator, ING Group, Amsterdam
- Professor Eric Thorne, Regional Co-ordinator, Australian Institute of Management
- Janine Colaes, Yvette McGree and Sheila O'Hare, Management Centre Europe, Brussels
- Count Konrad Goess-Saurau, Chairman, British Ceramic Tile, Allan Christopher, our CEO and all my fellow directors, at BCT, who are a such a stimulating and exciting team to work with.

People within my own field of organizational behaviour, who contribute to my learning and flow of adrenalin – and with whom it is always a great pleasure to work are:

- Professor Jim Dowd, Harvard Business School, formerly of IMD Business School, Lausanne
- Professor Mary Rose Greville, The Trinity Institute, Dublin and formerly of IMD, Lausanne
- Carita Wahlberg, Senior Training Manager, Stora Enso, Helsinki and Stockholm
- Alexey Wrykov, Training Manager, StaraEnso, St. Petersburg
- Peter Hanke, Director, Centre for Arts and Leadership, Copenhagen Business School
- Philippe Harberer, Director, SLT, Chamonix and Paris
- Chris Thomas, Senior Partner, Oxford PharmaGenesis
- Professor André Vandermerwe, formerly of IMI, Geneva and IMD, Lausanne
- Professor John Adair, for his limitless wisdom, unique insight and common sense perspectives

And my colleagues with whom I regularly collaborate in research, consultancy and leadership development, on many international assignments – and whose company I so enjoy:

Hilary and Barry Smith, Hermann Fischer, Judith Lorick, Messaouda Djoher, Stefano Bianchin, David Smith, Ian McMonagle, David Bowen, Glyn Jones, Richard Boot, Sonja Vissinga, Steve Crowther, Tom Cummings, Prof. Yury Boshyk and Dr Patrick Dixon.

It is with much affection and appreciation that I put on record my thanks to my editors and mentors, Angela Spall and Neill Ross, from Thorogood, for their help and guidance and, of course, to Neil Thomas, Thorogood's Chairman, for suggesting the book's title and for his valued friendship over the last fifteen years.

The experiences gained serving in British Special Forces undoubtedly have had a profound influence on both my perception and practice of leadership and I will always remain grateful for those early years, in my career, spent in the company of unforgettable colleagues and friends. It is, in part, from this rich experience that I have developed the concept of – *'Close-quarter Leadership'*.

Finally, it is to Brenda my wife, Countess Susie Goess-Saurau, our daughter and Professor Jonathan Williams, our son, that I express my heartfelt thanks for the invaluable day-to-day challenge to my thinking, fresh, exciting perspectives and gratuitous ego-deflation, that they each so willingly provide!

Contents

Introduction

Managerial wisdom probably begins with the recognition that there is no one 'right' style of leading or managing.

Leadership, especially, is very much about doing what is right for the situation and the people involved in it. Underlying such flexibility and differentiation of response, however, must be a consistency of values and ground rules, if the leader's professional credibility is to remain the crucial source of influence.

Credibility, in turn, in the role of a leader, goes beyond professional consistency and competence. Increasingly, in today's world, personal integrity, too, is coming to be regarded as a critical factor, as the *triple* bottom line of profitability, concern for the environment and, thirdly, social responsibility, becomes an established business imperative. Two recent significant, but unconnected, surveys – one in the USA and one in Europe – both indicated that being able to trust their leaders was the number one expectation of respondents. In each case, over 80% of replies identified trustworthiness as the necessary top leader attribute. As Professor John Adair states – *"Our position as a manager is confirmed by the organization, but our role as a leader is ratified in the hearts and minds of those whom we lead"*.

Such ratification is not simply a question of – do you believe the leader? Rather, it is one of – do you believe IN them? In turn, that belief is based upon what the leader is seen to deliver and achieve and how they are seen to behave.

Frequently described as – *"the most discussed, yet least understood"* aspect of management, leadership will, no doubt, continue to generate debate, exploration and analysis, so long as people inhabit the earth. "Are leaders born, or are they made?" is, similarly likely to remain a fundamental issue in that continuing discussion. Such a binary 'either – or' question, however, is deceptively simple and unnecessarily impedes understanding, by restricting our exploration of other critical factors, in our study of leadership and leaders.

Reviewed experiences, over many years, in various leadership roles and in a variety of very different arenas, undeniably confirms that the interplay of 'nature' and 'nurture' is the obvious core element in the development of personality and, therefore, leadership style. But it is also very much a matter of what *we do* with the hand of cards that we have been dealt and what we, as individuals, make of ourselves, by continually learning from our experience and the consequent *self-development* and professional renewal, for which we are each personally and ultimately accountable.

The question that lies at the root of leader acceptance is – can *he/she* lead and will *they* support and follow? What, then, are the key issues that confirm and underpin the leader-supporter nexus? What is it about leaders – and their leadership style – that influences people to give willingly – or withhold – necessary support and commitment? Above and beyond charm, charisma, inspiration, democracy, autocracy, or reputation, what behaviours – or more specifically – what *competency clusters* seem to confirm leaders in their roles?

Working with over 2,500 directors and managers, within ten different companies, in the US and in both Western and Eastern Europe, during the period 1998 – 2004, suggests that the critical indicators of leader credibility and, therefore, supporter commitment, are:

1. Strong goal orientation

Consistently, throughout our surveys, **a maintained focus on critical goals and the effective mobilization and direction of team members in pursuing those goals,**emerged as one of the critical competency clusters expected of leaders. Frequently associated with this group of leader competencies is an active concern to set the right direction and establish a clear, aligned achievement ethic, within the functions and teams managed and led.

2. Transparent integrity

Primarily, this amounts to having clear values and principles about work and people – and sticking to them in day-to-day activity – especially when under pressure to deliver results. In current terminology, this includes 'walking the talk'. What appears to reinforce and project integrity are high personal authenticity and strong awareness of self and others, which are consciously and consistently acted upon.

3. Close engagement with others

This group of social competencies centres upon a marked ability to form – and maintain – sound relationships, while retaining professional individuality.This competency cluster includes specific skills such as active listening, influencing, giving feedback, coaching and mentoring. Essential to the engaging process, we found, were sustained positive attitudes on the part of the leaders, particularly in conditions of adversity or pressure. Much of the successful engagement often appeared to be in the form of informal, but structured oral networking, the aim of which was to build up necessary commitment and support for projects and assignments. The really effective leaders always seemed to add something to people – not take anything away – in their dealings with others.

4. 'Helicopter' (contextual) perception

Essentially, the ability to see higher and wider than the immediate problem, or situation and to be able to put issues quickly into perspective and context. Often accompanying that wider view of issues, comes a developed capacity to generate a far greater range of potential solutions.

5. Resilient resourcefulness

The ability to find ways around, or through, problems and to come up with new solutions. As part of the competency cluster, we frequently saw **a marked ability to catalyze energy and even inspiration, amongst others, to generate new ideas and answers.** A recurring, allied strength was **the readiness to throw the rule book out and think things through afresh.**

6. Personal 'horsepower'

A consistently key factor in leader credibility, emerging from our surveys, was perceived **organizational 'clout' and the ability to influence and manage 'upwards' and 'outwards'.** Leaders who were listened to by their bosses and who influenced those above them, were generally held in high esteem, within the US and European cultures in which we largely work.

7. Resonant communications

Most likely associated with the strong awareness that has its roots in high emotional intelligence, **structured communication, that was consciously designed to strike chords with people, emerged as another fundamental leader competency** in our surveys. Clearly, leaders practising such 'resonant' communication **put a great deal more disciplined thought into what, why, how and when information – and 'passion' – should optimally be transmitted and discussed (and with whom) compared with those who did not.**

We frequently came across apparently 'ordinary' managers doing quite extraordinary things as leaders and producing exceptional results with their teams, but we also repeatedly saw so many instances of where 'satisfactory' performance could quite easily have been raised to 'outstanding' levels, but for the want of intelligent, courageous and fully-engaged 'close-quarter' leadership.

What also emerged from observation and discussions was just how much potential and talent is lying fallow, or untapped, in so many organizations. As ever, it seems, the problem is not so much one of a shortage of talent – *but of a serious lack of those who know how to develop, use and manage talent,* in mobilizing people for results.

The aim of this book is to focus on the seven competency clusters that our work suggests are crucial in the effective functioning of leaders, in the world of business and to offer ways in which such understanding and 'do-how' might be further developed. The competencies, critical though they are, need to be exercised for optimum impact within an organization, as the outcomes of a *shared leadership mindset,* driven by at least five fundamental factors:

1. Personal consistency, discipline and integrity

2. Intolerance of mediocrity

3. A concern to build mutual trust

4. Focused passion for the business

5. Recognition of the critical importance of emotional intelligence, in leadership

To borrow a phrase from that great seat of learning, INSEAD Business School, the objective of the pages that follow is to help: *"to develop the leaders, who develop the people, who develop the business…"*

Michael Williams

ONE
Close-quarter leadership

"Leaders go first. They set an example and build commitment through simple, daily acts that create progress and momentum. Leaders model the way through personal example and dedicated execution"

JAMES KOUZES & BARRY POSNER

For anyone in a leadership role the defining moment of truth is – *"It's YOUR call. What are you going to DO?"* Becoming a fully paid-up member of the – *'By my deeds ye shall know me'* school of leadership would seem, therefore, to be an indispensable qualification for leaders who consciously acknowledge the central nature of their role.

'Say – do' credibility, based upon the timeless obligation of leadership by example – and delivery – remains at the very root of leader acceptability, influence and, ultimately, success. But it is not simply a matter of action for action's sake. Even more so, true leadership is about as distanced as it can be from its grotesque parody – 'macho management'. Too easily, under pressure for results, a leader can fall into the seductive 'activity trap', in the often mistaken belief that 'any action is better than no action at all'. Equally, the myth of urgency and the confusion about what is 'urgent' and what is crucial exerts its insidious pressure, as a leader may feel the presence of some sneaky 'sword of Damocles' hanging over his ever-vulnerable head.

Fear of failure, or ridicule, rather than the real demands of the situation, so frequently become the arbiter of leaders' decisions and actions – or the trigger for inconsistent and inappropriate leadership 'style'. The influential findings of recent research by people like Jim Collins[1] and, in the UK, by Jane Simms[2] suggest that the key behaviours of currently successful leaders tend to be – strong professional will, *but with personal humility*, high self-discipline, a preparedness to confront brutal reality, a focused concentration on the business, strong communication, but also an absence of narcissism, and – a largely low-key, low-profile approach.

Such findings appear to be at odds with traditional perceptions of effective leaders who are so often seen as – highly egotistical, 'charismatic', high-profile, colourful personalities.

As more rigorous research now seems to indicate, some of those narcissistic leaders, who set out to cultivate mythology about themselves, have their 'brief, gaudy hour' and may achieve short-term successes, while others may bring about necessary turn-around within their businesses. Yet, not too many of them leave legacies of long-term transformation and *enduring* success.

As Collins says: *"…boards of directors frequently operate under the false belief that they need to hire a larger-than-life, egocentric leader to make a business great…"*. In support of that view, Simms makes the point that, the emergence of so-called 'low-key leadership' is partly a reaction against the CEO celebrity boom of recent years, where 'heroes' can turn into 'villains' overnight, dragging their companies down with them. Enron, Parmalat, WorldCom, Martha Stewart Living, Omnimedia, Andersen Consulting and Equitable Life being recent high profile examples of top executive greed, or financial gross misconduct. Simms further states: *"The greater focus on corporate governance is curtailing the power of the individual and humility is replacing the pre-Enron megalomania."*

This is not a plea for self-emasculating, over-compliant non-entities, but rather an acknowledgement of something capable leaders have always recognized, namely that success in most walks of life – and especially so in business – is usually the result of well-led teamwork, rather than the star performance of one charismatic egomaniac. Kriss Akabusi MBE, triple Olympic medallist and CEO[3], writing in Director, cites the Greek football team's triumph, in the 2004 World Cup and comments *"Greece demonstrated how teamwork could achieve far more than individual brilliance. Before the tournament began, the teams with flamboyant players were predicted to win. But as it progressed, it was clear that those teams who worked for each other were the ones winning the matches"*.

Time and again, observation and research in the ten companies[4] referred to in the introduction to this book, confirmed the ability to engage, mobilize and focus *others'* brain-power, energy and commitment as being core activities of those in leadership roles.

Leading at close quarters

Engaging, mobilizing and focusing people so often means opening up possibilities for them that they may not even know about. More than that, it involves making them feel that they have no limits – or, as Benjamin Zander[5] says: *"taking them beyond the bloody impossible"*.

A manager who remains addicted to the safe and familiar and who consistently fails to look afresh – and objectively – at challenges, is hardly likely to inspire others to listen for the sounds that are more powerful than the voice that says "no". That may be acceptable in businesses which unconsciously support the practices of 'reverse Darwinism' – survival of the weakest. It is not the mindset of a leader dedicated to creating an environment where people do what they are best at and continually excel in work they believe in passionately. Fundamental to such a mindset is the imperative of getting to know thoroughly – and engage fully with – each member of the team, in order to build trust and confidence and help them to deliver to the very best of their ability. This is essentially what 'close-quarter' leadership is about.

There are infinitely variable and diverse approaches to close-quarter leadership, depending upon the circumstances and the people involved in a particular situation.This does not mean that it can mean all things to all people because, within the criteria of *variability* and *diversity*, the process of full engagement is paramount – but it is also a uniquely personal process. To that end, close-quarter leadership may involve delegation, challenge, developing 'buy-in', coaching, nurturing and/or directing, as appropriate, but the *common threads* of creating a climate for learning, improvement – and *results* – will include, variously:

- *Setting and re-affirming direction, with as much emphasis on the 'why', as the 'what' and 'where to'.*

- *Increasing others' awareness of personal responsibility, role-commitment and ownership of results.*

- *Providing the stimulus to explore ways to think and behave differently and do things better.*

- *The opening up of opportunities for challenge and 'stretch', though new roles, job-enrichment, high-profile projects and testing assignments.*

- *Encouraging people to experiment or take initiatives and break from the past, where necessary.*

- *Empowering – and the often allied process of enabling – to build confidence and facilitate accountable action.*

- *Providing an environment where failure is acceptable, but where rapid learning from mistakes and the ability to recover and move forward are the expected norm.*

- *Perhaps, above all – active listening, directed feedback and regular opportunity for 'quality' dialogue.*

- *From the above close-quarter engagement – personal and professional growth of the leader, as well as the team members.*

Close-quarter leadership is about leading from behind, just as much as it is a matter of leading from the front. As the Marquis de Lafayette, one of France's greatest 'soldiers' generals', said: *"I am their leader, therefore I must follow them"*, meaning that he saw his role, as leader, as primarily that of someone responsible for doing all that he could, to *enable* his troops to excel and succeed.

Leading effectively at close quarters also means that the leader is, more often than not, there to *serve* team members – not merely be the 'boss' – in enabling them to cope successfully with the challenges of expected results. In such a context, the leader's power base becomes essentially *authoritative* – the *authority of expertize and competence* – not simply *authoritarian*, while the major source of *influence* stems from behaviour, 'style', consistency and trustworthiness.

Leaders' power, traditionally, is seen as having its roots, variously, in:

1. **Positional authority** – that of role, job, or status and the extent of authority conferred by superiors, in terms of available resources, budget, headcount and decision parameter.

2. **Expertize** – vested in a person's competence, in-depth or specialist knowledge and skills, or particular – often unique – expertize and abilities.

3. **Information** – access to facts, data and information, often exclusive, or privileged, that enhance an individual's influence and power, personally and/or professionally.

4. **Relationships** – so-called 'referral power', based upon cultivated alliances and connections with those in positions of power and influence, who are prepared to give 'political' support or sponsorship.

5. **Commitment** – people support and own what they create and the 'territorial' commitment that arises out of a sense of personal ownership gives a person power.

6. **Integrity** – an individual's trustworthiness, honesty and both personal and professional credibility give them 'moral authority', i.e. they are *identified with* possessing the moral high ground in a decision or event.

7. **'Personal Power'** – arises out of an individual's unique 'persona', presence and 'style' and the ways in which they influence, interact with, or dominate others. Includes 'charisma', vitality, raw energy, 'dynamism' and temperament.

As with any other form of leadership, those capable of leading for effect, at close quarters, will at some time draw upon all seven sources of power, be they ascribed, bestowed, derived, assumed, or otherwise acquired. In close-quarter leadership, especially, it is both the timing – as well as the *appropriateness* – of the use of leader power that is critical. Awareness of self and others, sensitivity and high empathy, the hallmarks of so-called *emotional intelligence*, emerge as crucial attributes in the exercise of power – especially in the conscious use of power, in whatever form – for optimal effect. Managing people, where c*ommunicating the right message – at the right time* is critical to requisite understanding and commitment – to the achievement of goals – means that the most appropriate *channels* must be used to ensure:

- The message is transparent, resonant – and is fully registering with the receiver.

- The intended signal is clear and as free from emotional 'noise' and clutter as it can be.

- The respective quality of transmission and reception are 'in sync', so that the receiver hears and feels what he/she is *intended* to hear and feel.

- There is 'buy-in', not by-pass.

When the relationships are face-to-face and leadership is literally at close quarters, the challenges of clear, unequivocal communication are difficult enough. When 'transmitter' and intended 'receivers' are regularly out of each others' sight, the risk of miscommunication multiplies infinitely. Two tools which can significantly reduce the chances of communication going awry, but especially at close quarters, are:

1. The communication **Stimulus – Response model** which identifies the linkage between the *nature of an interaction and the intended consequent outcomes of that interaction.*

2. The **Peak Communication concept** emerges out of the idea of *a hierarchy of communication and social intimacy, whereby both interpersonal payoff – and risk – increase, the further up the hierarchy we choose to operate.*

In more detail, these two processes are described, respectively, in figures 1 and 2, below.

NATURE OF INTERACTION ◄——————► **OUTCOMES OF INTERACTION**

(Stimulus)   (Response)

1. Cognitive   **Connects intellectually**

The 'factual information' channel: Descriptive, interpretative, objectively evaluative, with no emotional 'baggage'. Principal characteristics of this channel are – facts, logic, objective analysis and conclusion, rational thinking, realism

2. Emotional/affective   **Engages others' feelings and needs**

This channel involves the communication of values, feelings and emotions, e.g. – 'passion' for a business, or goal Principal characteristics are – subjectivity, personal feelings, beliefs, values and needs

3. Energy/inspiration   **Hooks hopes and aspirations**

The 'I-will-lead-you-to-a-better-world' channel, which focuses on hopes of a brighter, greater future Principal characteristics are – personal/professional aspirations and ambitions, indicative of wishes for a better life

---

NATURE OF INTERACTION ◄─────► OUTCOMES OF INTERACTION	
(Stimulus)	(Response)
4. Insight/wisdom	**Releases talent and potential**
The channel of communication which focuses others' sense of direction, purpose, goals and strategies Principal characteristics are – context and perspective, valid options/alternatives and the questions – 'why?' and 'why not?' and 'how best to…..?'	

FIGURE 1: CLOSE-QUARTER LEADERSHIP: STIMULUS AND RESPONSE
– THE NATURE AND QUALITY OF INTERACTION

Focusing people's thinking and actions lies at the heart of leadership and each of the four communication channels has its part to play in that process. Each channel, used with intelligence and developed awareness, invests communication, as appropriate, with factual authority, passion for a goal or rightful cause, a compelling vision of what is possible, or much needed fresh insights, when a solution seems impossible. Misused, or manipulated destructively, facts become distorted or corrupted, positive emotions succumb to cynicism, bigotry – or worse. Vested interests masquerade as moral principles and the fine line between vision and hallucination disappears, as fantasy assumes control and restrictive stereotyping stultifies creativity, innovation – and progress. Perhaps most important of all, is the recognition that these differing channels for communicating with others do exist and to know which to use – *and when* – for optimum resonance and impact, as a leader responsible for focusing people's thoughts and mobilizing their contributory energy and activity.

Whereas the communications process depicted in figure 1 describes the *messaging channels* available in transmitting and receiving information and knowledge, figure 2, below, identifies the extent of *interactive opportunities* open to us, in communicating and building productive relationships with others. Because of what are often felt to be personal risks – looking foolish, making mistakes, leaving oneself vulnerable, or being disadvantaged in some way – so many leaders (and others!) *regularly* miss the opportunities offered, when communicating at the highest levels of interaction. Frequently, our observations showed that fear of rejection and other forms of social 'punishment', outweighed the potential benefits and advantages, for influencing others, to be gained by taking the risks involved, at levels 4, 5 and 6 in the 'Communication and Interaction Hierarchy'. So often, the challenge to go higher and operate at *'peak communication'* levels, to open up opportunities for productive synergy, was met with that most destructive of all rebuffs – *'yes, but...'*

By no means a 100% culturally dependent issue, a general reticence to move beyond level 3 – into areas of *personal uniqueness* – was met working with managers from the UK, the US, Canada, most of Western Europe and also with those from Eastern Europe. The exceptions to the pattern tended to come, in the main, from younger men and women, already in key leadership roles, from various national cultures, who were often MBA graduates from *leading* Business Schools, or were comparably well-qualified professionals. They possessed a refreshing directness, which sometimes needed 'softening', in order to persuade others to respond in the same 'open', clear terms, free from emotional clutter.

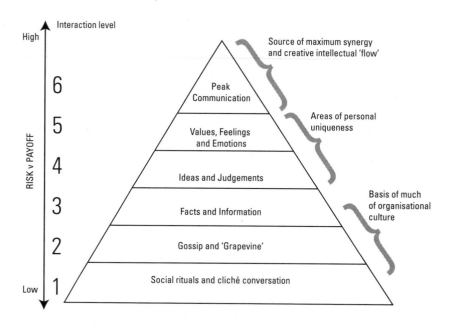

FIGURE 2: HIERARCHY OF COMMUNICATION AND INTERACTION

The model's origins are obscure, but it was extensively developed in the UK by David Gilbert-Smith, the Chief Executive of the Leadership Trust, together with his wife Janet, at Weston-under-Penyard, as one of several unique, 'bespoke' behavioural models, to provide context, focus and 'shape' to the powerful learning experiences, on the Trust's many world-class leadership training programmes.

In day-to-day management, where leading teams – and individuals – at close quarters is a matter of course, the concept of an interaction 'hierarchy', indicating progressively closer profitable engagement between people, helps to orientate and focus leadership style. Level 6 in the hierarchy represents, for practical purposes, the area of greatest *productive* interaction between people. It is where *synergy* and *shared* *'flow'* create the *collective* intellectual and emotional energy necessary for outstanding contribution and job performance.

'Peak communication' – where people alternately share, stimulate and jointly build ideas and solutions together – also provides the necessary positive arena, that allows for constructive challenge and disagreement. Between leaders and supporters who regularly engage in dialogue, at level 6, there is an easy spontaneity which facilitates productive debate and the readiness to introduce and explore options and alternatives, as *an automatic consequence of just being together.*

Interacting at such a degree of closeness, where there is little or no serious emotional 'baggage' impeding dialogue, requires high levels of honesty, forthrightness and mutual trust, as well as commitment to achieving the task on hand. High mutual awareness and respect, and a preparedness to subordinate self-interest to the needs of the team, or group, are also critical elements in achieving the fruitful synergy so typical of level 6 communication and interaction.

The actual moments when peak communication occurs, whereby ideas are *jointly* built upon, developed and carried forward to the action stage, cannot be legislated for. Such synergy occurs *naturally* in relationships where there is little concern about recrimination, little fear of failure or threat of rejection. What can be learned, introduced and consciously practised are the tools and techniques that reflect a leadership mindset which is concerned to develop and use peak communication, as a crucial means of getting the best out of people.

Some of the main keys to creating an environment and climate, in which peak communication and close engagement become regular possibilities in a relationship, include:

1. Find the shared 'connectors' that are critical to both (all) parties – i.e. the important common concerns, hopes, fears and goals.

2. Focus attention first on the other person(s) and their ideas, wants, values and concerns.

3. Look at the other person – NOT through, around, or over them.

4. Naturally match, or 'mirror', the other person's body language and posture (this implies approval, responsiveness, concern and interest – i.e. positive reactions).

5. Use 'we' and 'you', not 'I' – centred words and phrases.

6. Use language patterns that match those of the others, without submerging your own identity.

7. Value and show respect for the differences that exist between you. Remember! synergy comes from diversity, not uniformity, so look for the complementary strengths.

8. Explore the differences between you to find the common ground and the best mutually acceptable way forward (where the route to progress is not mandatory).

9. Constantly build upon what the other person is saying and help them, in turn, to add value to your ideas. Remember the positive role of – "Yes, and..." and the destructiveness of – "Yes, but..."

Emotional intelligence – the basis of close-quarter leadership

Both our own research – and that of many others in the field – has confirmed the central importance of emotional intelligence in leaders' behaviour and the development of leadership style. Just as there are measures of cognitive intelligence (IQ) so, in emotional intelligence, there is the parallel yardstick of EQ, which is defined as:

> The capacity for recognizing our own feelings and those of other people, for motivating and energizing ourselves and others and for managing emotions effectively, in ourselves and in our relationships.'

Given that definition, the importance of high EQ in close-quarter leadership, especially, becomes clear. Observation suggests that very emotionally intelligent managers and leaders, typically:

- Generate positive emotions in their relationships with others.
- Sense and discern the important underlying issues in interactions.
- Readily create a climate of goodwill.
- Build sound relationships through awareness, empathy and consistency.
- Exercise influence, through personal and professional integrity.
- Get things done, through the engaged commitment of others.

High EQ does not equate with stifled or suppressed emotion, neither does it mean that those possessing it are naturally 'soft' and lacking in what Tichy[6] calls *'edge'*, which is the 'steel', essential to taking necessary tough decisions. What seems to mark out those with high EQ, as being different, is that they can – and *do* – use considerable cutting edge, whenever they need to, but they use their steel constructively and positively, without rancour and not as 'punishment'. Typically, they:

- Have clear principles and values and stick to them.
- Exercise strong self-discipline in their judgement and decisions.
- Are manifestly consistent and honest.
- Challenge and disagree, but in a spirit of enquiry, exploration, progress – and learning.
- Can be creatively abrasive, in order to provoke new/different thinking and action.
- Engage in critical conversations and searching dialogue, to establish shared meaning and commitment prior to taking decisions.

and, in so doing, engage others – even in disagreement, or conflict – in peak communication.

As Dr Mike Bagshaw[7] of the Consultant Group 'Trans4mation' states:

"These emotional competencies have been shown to have a positive effect in business performance, over and over again. And organizations are beginning to sit up and take notice."

Perhaps in the spirit of *'Who cares wins'*, Bagshaw and his colleagues have developed a useful emotional intelligence mnemonic – **C.A.R.E.S.**, which has high relevance in close-quarter leadership.

Summarized, but especially from a leadership standpoint, the concept **C.A.R.E.S.** takes the following form:

C – Creative tension

This is a process of managing the inevitable pressures and tension between the situation as it currently is – and how we need it to be. It involves recognizing that many of the tensions surrounding necessary change are both inevitable – and legitimate – and identifying the most constructive, productive ways, to work through them – not dismiss them as irrelevancies – to manage today better, in order to get to an envisaged tomorrow.

A – Active choice

It means making decisions where there are several options available to us and where there are consequent competing risks and doubts. Choosing one course of action usually means that we are forced to forego others and rejecting some advantages that we prefer. Emotionally intelligent leaders appear to be able to come to a decision – involving risk and choice – and move on, without hankering after what has been lost.

R – Resilience under pressure

What so often lowers group morale, motivation and the will to overcome adversity, is not so much the difficulties facing the group as *the leader's perceived attitude towards the challenge and his/her ability and resolve to deal with it.* Nowhere, in leadership is this more immediate – and apparent – than when leading a team at close quarters.

E – Empathic relationships

Empathy means having the capacity and readiness to step into other people's shoes and see things from *their* point of view, with *their* perspectives and priorities. Empathy – like awareness of self and others – lies at the root of emotional intelligence and would seem to be a critical factor in successfully engaging closely and meaningfully with others.

S – Self awareness

This means being aware of how we feel and react in different situations. It is about knowing our strengths and our weaknesses and acknowledging the things that we both like and dislike about ourselves – especially in our dealings with other people. Self-awareness is not about self-obsession, nor is it self-consciousness. Rather, it is the necessary, *realistic* foundation to self-confidence and the preparedness to learn, develop and move forward in life – and as a leader.

An important distinction about emotional intelligence is that it *can* be learned and enhanced which, arguably, differentiates it from cognitive intelligence and so-called IQ.

This does not mean changing your *personality* – nor doing a DIY 'spin-doctor' job, to re-invent yourself – yet again! As Jo Maddocks (8) of JCA (Occupational Psychologists) says: *"The important question is – how can I be more effective? The answer is NOT to change who you are, but to learn how to manage yourself and your relationships better."*

Many successful leaders, in interview, during the ten-company surveys, stated that they never stop learning about leadership and management. Most cited seemingly small incidents, that occurred during the course of the working day, as frequently being the richest sources of their continuing learning and growth as leaders. One senior Dutch banker made the point that simply remembering to say 'thank you', using the person's first name and looking them in the eye, as he said it, had given a significant 'lift' to his relationships with his team members and colleagues.

An Austrian manager, in a major Italian insurance group, said that, for him, asking people for their recommendations on important issues and solutions, rather than simply telling them what and how to do their jobs, had been a very necessary and critical learning experience. Other respondents made the point that their key learning, as leaders, centred around often quite simple issues such as:

- Always keeping promises made and therefore only making commitments that they knew they could and would keep.

- Stating clearly "this is what **we** have to do" – NOT – "**they** have decided we have to..."

- Being prepared to take the blame and say to their own staff (and others) "Sorry, I got it wrong".

- Asking their team members – "What do you need me to do, to help you to.....?".

- Not asking their people to do things that they, as the manager, were not prepared to do.

- Not 'cherry picking' the choicest jobs for themselves and delegating the dull ones to their staff.

- Ensuring that team members received due acclaim and praise publicly and not 'stealing' the resultant kudos, for themselves, as the manager.

- Regularly creating opportunities for mutual feedback, dialogue and coaching, and actively managing people's performance.

- Encouraging reverse coaching, i.e. – team members coaching their boss on key issues.

- Where conditions allow, taking time out to 'walk and talk' with team members, using the outdoors as a conducive medium for discussion about sensitive or 'difficult' matters.

- Despite obvious time pressures, consciously making themselves more available to their people.

- Leadership by example arose time and again, as a key learning point, typified by the comments of a top investment banker from Chicago who said – "If I failed to walk the talk, just once, my team would never let me forget it. If I did it a second time, I'd be dead, as their boss".

Observations in the ten companies repeatedly confirmed the simple fact that leadership is not about slavishly following some theoretical 'style', or fad, but recognizing what is under our noses and dealing with it intelligently. The leader with high EQ is someone who picks up more readily, more deftly and with greater acuity, than others:

- Sensitive, urgent or significant issues that need to be dealt with and should not be ignored.

- Areas of potential conflict that need to be carefully surfaced and resolved.

- Less than obvious connections that suggest opportunity or productive potential.

- Gaps in communication and relationships that either need to be leapt over – or effectively filled.

- Veiled, subtle, or hinted at interactions that, if sensitively developed and progressed, could prove to be winning connections or relationships.

As Cooper and Sawaf[9] state in their excellent book – *Executive EQ:*

"Emotional intelligence is the ability to sense, understand and effectively apply the power and acumen of emotions as a source of human energy, information, connection and influence."

EQ is, in effect, the basis of the emotional 'alchemy', so critical in close-quarter leadership, that is about:

1. Going the 'extra mile' – and more than halfway – in initiating, building, or mending relationships.

2. The readiness to embrace uncertainty – particularly productive uncertainty, in taking decisions.

3. The preparedness to move out of 'comfort zones' and to take risks, in order to move things forward.

4. Using intuition, or 'sixth sense', in going against the rulebook, or convention that is no longer appropriate and realistic.

5. Expressing necessary constructive dissatisfaction and a readiness to change a state of affairs.

6. The courage to go first into the 'land-of-I-don't-knows', that lies beyond known, familiar territory.

7. Leading in a spirit of exploration, experimentation, creative innovation and enterprize.

As Maya Angelou says: *"To live is not just to survive, but to thrive with passion, compassion, some humour and style."*

Leaders with high EQ and 'Cutting Edge'

Leaders can lead – after a fashion – simply by downloading habitual ways of thinking and acting, but their influence and achievements are likely to be, at best, mediocre. Rarely, however, will they initiate the necessary *breakthroughs*, to move their worlds forward. Even less will they exploit and capitalize upon them. They are likely, too, to lose the plot as leaders – because they probably won't even have recognized it in the first place.

This is what Tichy refers to as the 'ultimate failure of leadership' – the lack of acuity, focus and disciplined edge, and the failure to recognize and respond effectively to the real challenges of their environment. He cites Arnold Toynbee's [10] example of nations and societies failing, or succumbing, once they have reached a *'condition of ease'* and have lost the will, cutting edge and self-determination to face reality and deal decisively with it.

Leaders of high EQ, with the necessary will, focus and 'steel', give the organization the speed, decisiveness, boldness and raw energy to break the boundaries of conventional wisdom, add necessary crucial value to the business – and its people – and move them forward. Their economic decisions will focus on where to invest time, money and resources for optimum payback and where – and how best – to add value to the business. Their 'people' decisions, aligned to the needs of the business, will face the realities of people's jobs, contributions, careers and futures. In Jim Collins' terminology, they will face the brutal facts, as disciplined leaders and, using a combination of professional will – and personal humility – they will get the right people on the bus, in the right places. Equally, they will get the wrong people off the bus, to set the right standards, take the right actions and start to achieve outstanding results.

Successful leaders who commit to – and deliver – outstanding results, do so as a result of the effective leadership and management of their *teams*. They understand that their route to success is, inevitably through engaging, focusing and mobilizing *others'* brainpower, horsepower and commitment.

Leadership is about taking people beyond what they thought they were capable of – and creating jobs, roles, relationships and an environment whereby people can excel in work that uses and extends their talents, and about which they feel passionate. To do that, leaders need to engage closely and fully with those whom they are charged with managing and leading. In becoming effective close-quarter leaders, managers, more than at any other time, will be leading by example and will be exercising power and influence which are highly personal, as much as they are professional and authoritative. Such engaged, close-quarter leadership relies for its impact and success upon consistently clear, resonant communication. Necessarily, this involves:

1. Recognizing and appropriately using *all* the right communication *channels*, at the right times.

2. Understanding, acknowledging and using all levels of the *'Hierarchy of Communications'* and being able to operate, at will, with others at so-called 'peak communication' levels, to stimulate necessary productive interaction and creative synergy.

The most important clues about what to change, or improve – and how best to do it – are there, day-to-day, right under our noses. Developing the necessary discriminatory perceptiveness, acuity and the ability to 'sense' when, or when not, to intervene, is central to professional and personal growth, as a leader and manager. It is a matter of developing the right mindset, as well as the right skills. It is essentially a selfless, not a narcissistic process, where the main focus is upon the team and its members, the organization and the results that are critical to ensuring the future of the company.

Change the leadership mindset – and you change the whole business.

As Rijkman Groenink, Chairman of ABN AMRO[11] the highly successful global bank, says:

"Effective leaders are leaders with the strength and courage to change themselves, to grow, while retaining their essential self. If its leaders have the ability to change and grow, so will the organization."

Chapter one references

1. Collins, J. Good to Great, Random House Business Books

2. Simms, J. *Leadership – Low Profile Bosses*, Director, Vol 57, No. 7, 2004; Institute of Directors

3. Akabusi, K. Letter, Director, Vol 58, No 1, 2004; Institute of Directors

4. 10 Companies in US, Canada, (food) Western Europe, (Wood pulp, Chemicals, pharmaceuticals, banks, insurance, electricity, service). Eastern Europe, (service, pharmaceuticals) Author's collaborative research, 1998-2004

5. Zander, B. Lanseer Productions, BBC TV, The Works *Living on one Buttock*

6. Tichy, N. *The Leadership Engine*, Harper Collins, 1997

7. Bagshaw, M., Trans4mation Consultants, *So what is EI? Wiltshire Business*, October 2003

8. Maddocks, J., JCA Occupational Psychologists, *Emotional Intelligence*, Wiltshire Business, October 2003

9. Cooper, R. K. & Sawaf, A. *Executive EQ*, Perigee, 1998

10. Toynbee, A, quoted in Tichy, N. Ibid

11. ABN AMRO Chairman's statement on management development document

TWO
Leadership theories, role models – and common sense

*"There is nothing so practical as
a theory that works"*

PROFESSOR BARRY TURNER

*"Business leaders have the difficult
task of acting as role models every
hour of every day"*

ANDREW BROWN

The world of business is essentially one where applied, intelligent common sense, allied to the outstanding management of people, money, resources and information, are seen as the critical executive strengths. It is primarily a managerial arena where pragmatism, productive 'do-how' and discipline – in the achievement of results – are regarded as the more laudable managerial virtues. In such a world of forecasting, planning, organization, mobilization and control, there is no gain saying the crucial importance of reality, practicality and sound common sense, as key executive competencies.

Almost by default, pragmatism has inevitably assumed the dominant role, in relation to theory, in the practices of management and leadership, within the vast majority of organizations that make up the business world. In recognition of that position of precedence and preference, it must be said that the management philosophies and so-called practices taught at many business schools, universities and by major consultancies, often bear little relation to the managerial realities of shop-floor leadership, cross-functional integrative management and corporate governance. Clearly, there *are* exceptions to this criticism. In the UK, Exeter University, Warwick, Cranfield, London and Ashridge are among those British business schools whose teaching *does* have its roots in reality, while INSEAD at Fontainebleau, IMD at Lausanne, Stockholm School of Economics, Copenhagen Business School and Nyenrode, in Holland, offer some of the most relevant – and creative – learning experiences available for business leaders, on a par with those of the best US business schools.

D. O. Hebb[1] an American psychologist, made the point that – "theory is a sophisticated statement of ignorance" and in providing learning opportunities for leaders – be they managerial training programmes, workshops, or face-to-face coaching – we need to remain conscious of Hebb's definition. Taking a different view, Professor Barry Turner[2] suggests there is nothing so practical as a theory that works. Theories that provides necessary context, perspective and understanding, to practice, offer people both meaning and a sense of purpose, which they might not otherwise find, by being excessively committed to utilitarian pragmatism.

A great many gurus have entered the very testing arena of business leadership and management, over the last hundred years. Their acceptance, survival and professional longevity have depended upon their ability to add *perceived* value to the body of knowledge, understanding and evolving best practices that represent state-of-the-art leadership and management.

Among those who have invested leadership theory with major significance are John Adair, Paul Hersey and Kenneth Blanchard, Noel Tichy, Warren Bennis, Henry Mintzberg, Charles Handy and, most recently,

Jim Collins. All have developed models or concepts of leadership, way beyond mere fad, that have stood – or will stand – the test of time. All have added major value to our understanding and practice of both leadership and management.

This chapter explores some of the practical and applicable ideas of Adair, Hersey and Blanchard, Tichy and Collins.

1. Professor John Adair

A former soldier and subsequently lecturer at the at the Royal Military Academy, Sandhurst. John Adair[3] held the first Chair in Leadership at a British university. A prolific author and public speaker, he has developed and promoted the concept of 'Action-centred leadership' shown in figure 3, below.

Action-centred leadership – the model and constructs

Adair's model of leadership is based upon three key functions of leaders, i.e.:

1. Achieving the task
2. Maintaining the team
3. Meeting the needs of the individual

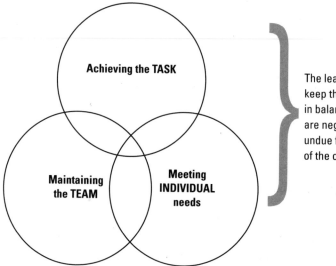

Achieving the TASK

Maintaining the TEAM

Meeting INDIVIDUAL needs

The leader's role is to keep the three functions in balance, so that none are neglected through undue focus on either of the others

FIGURE 3: THE ADAIR LEADERSHIP 'TRINITY'

Adair's model has been extensively used since the 1960's and is acknowledged as being a pragmatic and relevant basis for the day-to-day leadership and management of tasks, teams and individuals, at any level, from shop-floor to Boards of directors.

The central notion of *maintaining equilibrium of focus*, between – *meeting the demands of the task, maintaining the team and meeting the needs of individual team members* – is a major guide to leaders and provides a practical yardstick for self-monitoring, self-development, training and coaching. The model, as a whole, provides a relevant discipline in exercising close-quarter leadership and lends both form and focus to that highly engaged style of leading and managing.

2. Paul Hersey and Kenneth Blanchard

Early in the 1970's Hersey and Blanchard[4] developed their concept of *'Situational leadership'*.

The basic premise of their model is that the *functioning maturity of the team members* is a major determinant of the 'style' and focus that need to be adopted by leaders, in order to elicit the optimum productive responses from people.

'Functioning maturity' is the degree to which people are sufficiently:

1. Competent to successfully undertake the task given them

2. Confident to cope with the challenges posed by the task

3. Committed and motivated to undertake the task

Plotting a range of leadership styles, based upon 'appropriateness' of behaviour, against a comparable continuum of team member *functioning maturity*, from 'low' to 'high', the **Situational Leadership** model is shown in figure 4, below.

For example, leader style **S1** ('Telling') where the leader explains, tells, coaches, trains, as appropriate, is most likely to be the approach necessary to help team members to understand exactly what is expected of them, where their functioning maturity is low **(M1)**.

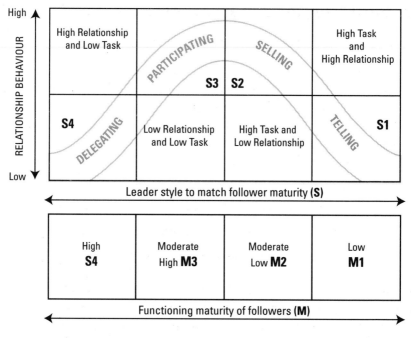

FIGURE 4: THE SITUATIONAL LEADERSHIP MODEL

Similarly, where the team members are all competent, confident and committed **(M4)**, then the appropriate leader style would be **S4** ('Delegating' and, one might add, empowering).

Had such a concept of leadership been understood – and *practised* – in the 'bad old days', at British Leyland, it might have prevented some of the ignorance, confused reactions and costly mistakes that followed one senior executive's public statement, at the company's then newest plant, composed largely of people with no experience of working in a car factory – *"With effect from April, we will adopt an open, participative style of management"* (i.e. level S3/S4).

April was two months off, the workforce was almost universally at a functional maturity level of M1 and, with few exceptions, most managers were operating, themselves, at levels M1 and M2.

Leadership, as such, was virtually non-existent and the operators had organized and marked off the areas under the overhead production line, as a succession of badminton courts, mini football pitches and spaces for other pastimes, during the frequent stoppages and consequent down-time. What was desperately needed, short-term, was some very effective S1 close-quarter leadership!

The Situational Leadership model is a relevant and practical tool. Like John Adair's 'three circle' concept, it can be used as another set of personal development benchmarks, in building and giving necessary form to managers' evolving leadership styles.

Equally, as with 'Action-centred leadership', the 'Situational leadership' model is widely known in the UK and using its logic as a basis for leader development is often a matter of revisiting previous learning. Furthermore, it is a concept that lends itself readily to the development of a common leadership language and practices *throughout an organization,* as does the Adair model.

3. Noel Tichy

Tichy[5] an American academic, who is well known for his study of trans-formational leadership (see chapter 3) and leader development of other leaders, evolved the concept of the **Leadership 'engine'**. His model is based upon the premise that leaders are essential, as the energizing and driving force in collective activity. Tichy sees leaders, necessarily, as committed, focused, tough individuals of high energy, who lead by example. Tichy regards the effective mobilization of people – including other leaders – as central to the leader's role and primary contribution to the organization.

The Leadership 'engine' has three distinct facets to it, as is shown in figure 5.

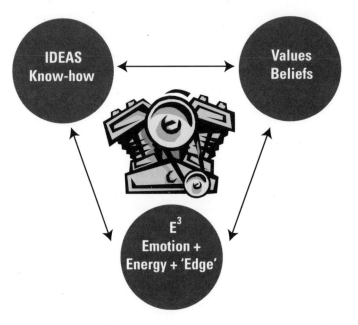

FIGURE 5: THE LEADERSHIP ENGINE

In more detail, the three essential components of Tichy's Leadership engine are:

1. **Leaders are responsible for ensuring that there are sufficient ideas and information flowing, that are relevant to the task on hand.** The leader's role may, variously, be to generate, stimulate, trigger, or foster new or fresh thinking on an issue, or problem. Leaders, themselves, are not the fount of all knowledge, but their task is to make sure that sufficient insight, intuition, logic and intellectual energy is made available to deal effectively with the challenges facing the team.

2. **In leading by example – 'walking the talk' – leaders provide a continual living demonstration of the values which represent the core culture of the team or group.** Day-to-day, through

integrity and consistency, their role is to define and exemplify what their group stands for and believes in.

In many cultures – including those which collectively constitute the British way of doing things – there can often be a fine and subtle line between integrity and pretentiousness. Usually those on the receiving end, sooner rather than later, distinguish the real thing from the inauthentic and spurious.

The third component is what Tichy defines as the E3 Factor. This, in turn, is made up of three elements:

- Emotion and drive to get the job done well.

- Energy and the ability to energize others and create energy and synergy where none existed previously.

- 'Edge' – which is the the ability to take necessary tough decisions and remain resolute and resilient, in conditions of adversity or high pressure. If leaders with 'edge' go down, they don't stay down, but rather live by a philosophy of – 'So, life gives you lemons – then make lemonade!'

In Tichy's terms, 'Edge' represents the difference in leadership style between those who will win – and those who will lose, in today's competitive world.

Leaders with edge give a business speed, decisiveness, boldness and 'raw' energy. Leadership edge can apply to decisions about where to invest time, money and resources, for optimum payback and where and how best to add value to the business.

Equally, edge may give the necessary reality to 'people' decisions, about individuals' performance, jobs, roles, careers and futures.

Edge is the very opposite of what Arnold Toynbee described as the *'condition of ease'* – in essence, a leadership 'plateau' of:

- lack of acuity, focus and sharpness

- Absence of a will to win

- Failure to recognize and respond effectively, in time, to critical challenges within their environment

As Tichy states – *"This is the ultimate failure of leadership..."*

4. Jim Collins

Author of the best-selling book, *Good to Great,* one-time McKinsey research analyst, former Stanford professor and proponent of the contro-versial *'first who... then what'* principle, Jim Collins[6] emerges as one of the most exciting and challenging of the current management gurus. His findings on leadership are as surprising as the conclusions that he came to about the ways in which 'good' companies achieve sustainable great-ness and he has evolved from his extensive research, in over 1400 companies, what he defines as *'Level 5 leadership'*.

Working by logical, incremental steps, in a highly disciplined and focused way, Level 5 leaders look first to get the right people onboard – and in the right roles (and get rid of the wrong people) before they ask the question 'what?'. In other words, their first priority is the right people and *then* they set the right direction. They are also consistent leaders with a strong sense of accountability and high 'say-do' credibility. Collins and his research team found that the so-called Level 5 leaders tended to work consistently and diligently, over considerable periods of time, at devel-oping a 'flywheel' effect, to create ever-increasing momentum, in transforming their companies from good to great. Collins identified several more unusual, or unexpected, characteristics, among the 'good-to-great' leaders, including a readiness to confront brutal and often unpalatable facts, such as, for instance:

> *"We're at least 20% over-manned in our manufacturing operations. Why?"*

"The pace, nature and direction of transformation of this organization have overtaken the HR manager's knowledge and competency levels and are way beyond her professional experience. There is no longer a place for her, in this seat, on this 'bus'. We must find a replacement, within 3 months."

"This supplier has successively taken us for a ride, for at least the last 18 months. As a result, we've incurred avoidable losses of over £350,000. How, precisely, did this happen?"

"Yield of first quality tiles, in production, has been running at around 73%, for the last 3 weeks, when it should have been consistently over 95%. What, exactly, do we need to do differently?"

Level 5 leaders focus just as much upon what they and the business need to STOP doing and what should be abandoned, as they do on what *new* practices and processes they need to adopt, in the interests of greatness. Shedding much loved brands, products and practices (often hallowed by little more than the passage of time) can be one of the toughest decisions that CEO's and their Boards have to make. These, too, are the decisions that demand that leaders persist and don't waver in the face of opposition and ridicule from those with vested interests in preserving the status quo.

Confronting hard reality and working through the 'Stop doing' list, moves a business closer to what Collins describes as the *'Hedgehog Concept'* and, in turn, provides a further logical basis for necessary transformation. *Hedgehogs provide the analogy because of their ability to recognize the one big, critical factor facing them and so they are able to break down the complex, and multi-facetted, into a fundamental and focused single idea* (as opposed to foxes, who know a great many varied and small things and may diffuse and spread their efforts too widely). Most good-to-great leaders it seems, from Collins' study, are 'Hedgehogs', rather than 'Foxes'.

In the form of another 'unholy trinity' (figure 6) the Hedgehog Concept is best portrayed as three intersecting circles, representing much needed, disciplined thinking, in the form of three pivotal questions:

- What can we be best in the world at? (and, equally important – what can we not be best at?)

- What is the economic denominator that best drives our economic engine, e.g. profit per 'x'?

- What are our core people deeply passionate about?

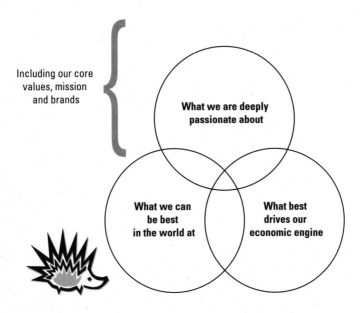

Including our core values, mission and brands

What we are deeply passionate about

What we can be best in the world at

What best drives our economic engine

FIGURE 6: THE 'HEDGEHOG CONCEPT'

Level 5 leaders, according to Collins' study are essentially disciplined people who lead through an unusual combination of *professional drive* (strong focus on the business – not themselves) and *personal humility* (as opposed to arrogance and egotism).

Figure 7 sets out the interplay of the two characteristics which underpin the principal good-to-great leadership style and focus.

'GOOD-to-GREAT' – what makes the difference?

'Level 5' Leaders lead by:

PROFESSIONAL DRIVE	**X**	**PERSONAL HUMILITY**
Create outstanding results		Show compelling modesty
Demonstrate unwavering resolve		Act with quiet determination
Set and maintain standards		Channel ambition into the company
Assume responsibility for poor results		Credit others with success

FIGURE 7: 'LEVEL 5' LEADERSHIP STYLE

All of the above models and concepts, from John Adair's 'Action-centred Leadership' to Jim Collins' 'Level 5 Leadership', provide practical insights into the functions, roles and processes which, together, make up organizational leadership. Each one offers something that virtually everyone, in a leadership role within the business world, can use as a basis for developing and enhancing their own competencies and style, as a leader – especially if they are prepared to take on the challenges of becoming a better close-quarter leader.

Close-quarter leadership, both as a mindset and as a series of carefully-honed practices, is so-described because the process depends upon high leader awareness, focus and commitment to others' success. The parties involved, necessarily, become professionally engaged, as closely as possible, with very clear intended aims and outcomes, that might not otherwise be achievable, through more 'distant', less focused leadership.

Such styles of leadership are best developed by:

- Coaching by a competent, experienced close-quarter leader with specific results-based feedback.

- Bespoke – as opposed to general – leadership training, with participant and tutor feedback.

- 'Reverse' coaching, where team members, on the receiving end of the individual's leadership, give him/her feedback and coaching on the felt impact of that leadership style.

- Regularly analyzed 'incident-method' self-review and feedback, facilitated, explored and constructively built upon by a trusted, credible third party.

- If and where available, appropriate role-models.

One problem is that there are, as yet, too few role-models of the kind needed to provide sufficiently credible examples, for others to follow and emulate.

The 'classical' leader role-models so often quoted – Mandela, Gandhi, Churchill, Richard Branson, Archie Norman, Lee Iacocca, or Jack Welch are all, in their differing ways, examples of great leaders. All are, or were, charismatic leadership icons on a grand scale – several of them being dynamic, larger-than-life personalities. A major factor with role-models is recognizing when such icons actively corrupt, or simply no longer *represent*, currently defining values, needs and realities. In other words, at which point – and why – would you cease to follow Hitler, General Custer, Napoleon, Ernest Shackleton, or even Winston Churchill?

Low-key 'thinking' leadership

As we saw in chapter one, however, currently emerging highly successful leaders, in the world of business, tend to operate in more low-key ways to achieve sustainable transformation and greatness, for their businesses. By and large, they don't fit the outgoing, extravert stereotype of the traditionally accepted leadership role-model. They are leaders of a different ilk, creating new, *involving* operational environments, where the cultural, economic and social imperatives that determine leadership ability and style are changing dramatically – where the traditional critical leader message – *"Follow me and I will lead you to a better world..."* becomes re-defined as – *"Together, we will build a better world..."* Among *their* key directional competencies are:

1. The ability to reduce complexity to profound and manageable simplicity.

2. Strong, clear sense of necessary direction.

3. The ability to identify the real priorities for concerted action.

4. Resolute single-mindedness in the dedicated pursuit of those priorities.

5. The acuity to ask the sort of questions that will ignite necessary change and transformation.

6. High awareness and insight in their ability to mobilize and move others in the direction required.

Such leaders typically *act* like thinking people, while they *think* like action-oriented individuals, focusing strongly on the requisite goals and outcomes of the business – not their own image and personal standing. However, there are some disadvantages – even dangers – in low-key, 'quiet' leadership styles. Deflecting interest away from themselves and into the business can make a leader appear as colourless, devoid of charisma and lacking in personality. Communication skills – and the related demonstrable ability to inspire others – remain as essential elements of a leader's expected repertoire of talents. Thus there is a fine line between *professional* low-profile leader styles that *do* deliver – and acquiring a reputation as a 'grey nonentity' who collects the rewards, while others, of higher visibility, are assumed to be doing all the hard work.

In her very cogent article – on the UK's more publicity-shy heroes, which appeared in the February 2004 edition of the Institute of Directors journal *Director* – Jane Simms[7] identified some of Britain's very successful 'dark horse' CEO's and Chairmen who generally shun the limelight. Most appear to avoid becoming cult figures, or media personalities, and focus their energies and commitment in very targeted ways on the business. Her impressive list includes Terry Leahy, CEO of the highly successful Tesco Supermarket chain, CEO John Peace, whose Company GUS outper-formed the FTSE All Share by 134%, since his appointment in 2000, Julian Richer, Chairman, Richer Sounds who is highly regarded by customers, investors and his own people alike and Rose Marie Bravo, CEO, Burberry, who has transformed an ailing brand the into a leading 'must have' fashion item, growing capitalization from £200 million to £1.4 billion, in just four years.

Maintaining a low profile and avoiding becoming an icon or symbol, when clearly successful and under public pressure to assume the role of a cult figure, may be difficult in the extreme. The City, the press – and business in general- want successful role-models and frequently add their own 'colouring matter' to make them appear larger than life. Manfred Kets de Vries, Professor of Leadership Development at INSEAD business school states – *"People project fantasies onto them and they become a walking symbol, which can be very hard to carry"*.

It is also very human and very natural to want to receive recognition and bouquets, in an age where brickbats and public criticism, often barely short of defamation, have become an established occupational hazard for CEO's and other senior business leaders. 'Good' publicity, and culti-vated leader 'brand image', can undoubtedly be good for the business and some low-profile leaders have been criticized for not projecting their personal profiles sufficiently, in the public interests of their companies.

Clearly, it is possible to lead effectively, in a low-key and very focused way, without unnecessary narcissistic 'baggage' contaminating the process and so taking the leader's eye off the critical ball. Leahy, Peace, Richer, Bravo and many others, are living evidence of the success of understated, but exceptionally talented, high-achieving leaders. Collins' research and Simms' findings – about leaders and leadership – would seem to reaffirm, on both sides of the Atlantic, Alexander Pope's adage:

"...Charms strike the sight, but merit wins the soul" – and, it would seem, ensures sustainable longer-term business success.

Experience and theory – a necessary synthesis

Nothing can entirely replace direct experience, as the most practical source of learning for leadership.

However, when a manager says – *"I've had 30 years' experience of leading and managing..."* we need to know if those were 30 years in which the most important lessons were continually drawn, explored and learned from. Or – was it one year's experience more or less repeated 30 times over?

Theory, which is relevant – *and which works* – lends context and perspective to experience and helps to provide critical links and insights which enhance, focus and give direction to learning. Moreover, theory may invest experience with a significance that otherwise might not be there.

As was stated in the Introduction to this book, leadership is currently one of the most discussed and yet least understood phenomena in the world of industry and business. The theories, constructs and models reviewed in this chapter are all offered as practical and essentially *complementary* tools for understanding more of the processes, skills and mindsets fundamental to sound leadership practice. Furthermore, used in conjunction, they provide insights into the *roles, functions and responsibilities* of leaders – and, therefore, some of the expectations people may legitimately hold of those who lead them. They are offered not as an 'either-or' selection of ideas, but as a collection of concepts and models which, together – and used selectively – provide a practical basis for *both progressive coaching and managed self-development*, for leaders

The first concept, John Adair's **Action-centred leadership** model, emphasizes the importance of keeping in balance, the leader's personal direction of effort between achieving task objectives, maintaining effective, aligned teamwork and mobilizing individual team members' commitment.

Hersey and Blanchard's **Situational leadership** model is based upon the leader's need to recognize – *and respond appropriately to* – the degree to which those involved can and will successfully achieve the task objectives facing them. Thus the leader's *style* needs to *match and complement* the functioning maturity of those being led.

Noel Tichy's **Leadership engine** highlights the importance of the *leader's contribution* to group performance, by generating/facilitating ideas and solutions, identifying and crystallizing necessary group values and, through what he terms the 'E-3' Factor, i.e. – leading with emotion (passion), energy and 'edge' (toughness).

The fourth model is that of Jim Collins, which he terms '**Level 5 leadership**'. According to Collins' extensive research, Level 5 leaders are essentially low-key, but disciplined thinkers who are dedicated to making their businesses great. They succeed as leaders through a combination of *high professional drive aimed at outstanding delivery – and personal humility*. They give due praise to others for success and take the blame when things go wrong. Rather like the philosophy of Wellstream Northsea, manufacturers of high quality steel tubing for the oil industry, Level 5 leaders appear to lead by a personal code of – *"We commit. We deliver – and there are no excuses"*.

Currently, much of the most relevant research into leadership 'best practice' consistently identifies *strong directional sense*, with its attendant skills of acuity, focus and the ability to identify the real priorities, as a critical competency 'cluster' of successful leaders.

Chapter two references

1. Hebb, D. O. *Quoted in Proceedings*, IMI Business School, IAMP, 1989 Geneva

2. Turner, B.T. *Proceedings*, Rover Cars in-house Management Programme, 1988

3. Adair, J. Action-Centred Leadership model, illustrated in many of Professor Adair

4. Hersey, P. & Blanchard, K. H. *Management of Organizational Behavior*, Prentice-Hall, 1977

5. Tichy, N. Ibid

6. Collins, J. Ibid

7. Simms, J.Ibid

THREE
Leadership and the achievement ethic

"Unfortunately, top people are often there because they are expert in what was important yesterday... We put more energy into developing skill sets, rather than the right mindsets"

PROFESSOR JONAS RIDDERSTRÅLE, STOCKHOLM SCHOOL OF ECONOMICS

"There must be a beginning of any great matter, but the continuing unto the end until it be thoroughly finished yields the true glory"

SIR FRANCIS DRAKE

In their major study into the attraction and retention of high-performing, talented people – '*The War for Talent*' – in the late 1990's, McKinseys found that companies which had cultivated a strong, high-achievement culture were frequently the winners in the 'war'. Unsurprisingly, their findings confirmed the obvious simple fact that capable, outstanding performers wanted to be in similarly high achieving organizations.

As crucial aspects of high achieving cultures, McKinsey identified 'great jobs', which allowed people both ample headroom and sufficient 'elbow-room', to use their talents and to excel, often for up to 80% of their time in their roles. One key factor associated with 'great jobs' was the presence

of comparably 'great managers', or great leaders, who provided sufficient support, autonomy and directed empowerment for their people.
Such managers, it seems, operate in the style of close-quarter leaders –
hands-off, but eyes and ears on – and committed to making optimum
use of the talent available to them.

Acknowledging the reality that autonomy in almost any organization is
a matter of *independence, within a network of interdependence,* close-
quarter leadership involves defining the parameters of what is essentially
'freedom within a framework'. Further, it requires leaders to enable
individuals – and teams – to operate to the very limits of the frameworks
and, indeed, to regularly test out the boundaries themselves, to validate
their continuing relevance to high achievement and progress.

The work of professor Tom Paterson
– a treasure unearthed

Some fifty-plus years before the McKinsey survey, Tom T. Paterson[1]
evolved a model aimed at *developing leadership of high performing teams*
– at that time, RAF fighter squadrons, whose morale had fallen significantly, after the heady, ultimately successful months of the Battle of Britain.
In his later years, Paterson became Professor of Organizational Behaviour
at Strathclyde University and introduced his ideas on leadership to the
business world.

Unfortunately, his use of somewhat arcane terminology (an uncomfort-
able mixture of classical Greek and Latin) was the probable cause of his
otherwise very relevant concepts simply not catching on in industry. Very
few machine-shop foremen, assembly shop managers (or, for that matter,
CEO's) are likely to identify whole-heartedly with the notion that they
are 'methectic' leaders, with both 'indominus' and 'exdominus' roles to
fulfil. Especially was this so in an age when 'quid pro quo' was generally interpreted on the shop floor as the going rate for a pre-Wolfenden

streetwalker, or optimistic shop stewards saw it as management's offer of an extra pound per week, all round! As a consequence, outside academic circles , the model was generally not taken as seriously as it deserved to be.

Put into plain English – or any other living language – and updated, Paterson's model makes good sense since it puts the leader at the *centre* of an interactive process, of high *interdependence*, for defining, managing and delivering requisite results, through other people. That centrality of role also underlines the potential for influence of the leader, in fostering and maintaining an achievement ethic, within the arenas of his/her responsibility. Furthermore, it is a degree of centrality – and, hence, influence – that can be reinforced and progressively consolidated, each time the leader acts in an engaged, close-quarter role. Thus, the option and the initiative to influence, or not, lie largely with the leader. The personal and professional context of that option, as always, is one of risk versus payoff.

Paterson's concept of leadership uses the classical *input – conversion – output* model of productive activity and achievement, shown in figure 8, below. In contemporary business practice, where the implications of *value-added* and *competitive/collaborative advantage* have critical significance, updating of the original model takes the form of an *'outcomes'* add-on.

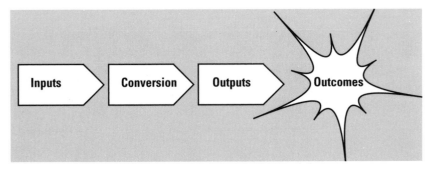

FIGURE 8

In this simple model, representing both sequence and consequence, 'inputs' may, for example be rough castings, 'conversion' could, therefore, be machining and assembly and 'outputs' would most likely be complete product units – for example – lawnmower engines. In turn, 'outcomes' could include customer satisfaction, an increased order book, higher profits and sustained growth of the business – all measures of requisite achievement.

As we export more and more of our manufacturing base to the East and increasingly become service providers, the input-output-outcome chain, more often than not, is one of data and information, in several forms, being converted into data and information in many more very different forms. Outcomes are then usually information intelligence and new understanding.

When the network of interdependence and leadership functions are imposed upon the model, it takes shape as a series of potential interactions and influences, with achievement as its central theme, as shown in figure 9.

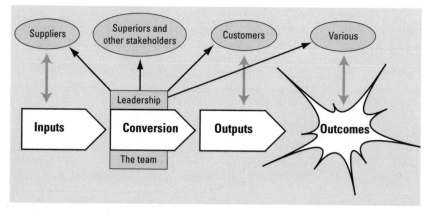

FIGURE 9

Leadership of any 'conversion' process, or stage, in the value chain necessarily involves influencing supplier responses, in order to ensure that the right inputs are available in the form and at the time needed. Bosses and other stakeholders in the process need to be managed effectively and regularly kept informed and customers and clients need to be supplied and serviced, according to contract.

Both desired and unintended outcomes, similarly, must be professionally initiated, developed and managed, to optimize the wider and longer-term *achievement* implications of 'conversion'.

In this network of function, roles and relationships, Paterson believed that at least **four** leadership roles needed to be performed, as and when conditions demanded. In addition, he saw a critical fifth *follower/supporter* role that was crucial to effective output – and successful outcomes.The four leadership roles are:

1. Inward leader role

The principal orientation and pre-occupation of this role is the 'internal' life of the team – its task performance, cohesiveness, morale, intrapersonal relationships, continual learning and development. The leader, in this role, is most closely engaged with the team members themselves and what needs to be done to energize and mobilize the group – or individuals – from *within* the team. Close-quarter dialogue concentrates upon 'you', 'me' and 'us' and the 'here-and-now'. The Inward Leader helps to define and crystallize the team's vision, mission, values and goals and to secure buy-in from the members to these and to other critical initiatives. The functioning maturity of the team – and of individual members – is a major concern of the Inward Leader, hence much of his/her focus involves ensuring *fitness for task and role,* of the work group, including the group's internal communications and information sharing.

2. Outward leader role

In this role the leader's concern is to develop and maintain effective, functioning relationships with key players in the team's external world; for example suppliers, customers (and customers' customers) superiors and other significant stakeholders whose activities impinge upon those of the team. Of particular importance is the clarity, quality and timeliness of the team's communication – and level of engagement – with its key external contacts.

The Outward Leader's role is to represent the team's best interests in various arenas and 'corridors of power', within the rest of the organization and also in the world at large. Their task is to align the team's aims and objectives with those of the organization and the wider context of its business. In the role of 'outward leader', lobbying on behalf of the team, appropriately promoting its successes, sponsoring and opening doors for members and building bridges for collaboration and synergy with other functions or units, are all typical close-quarter leadership activities, designed to integrate the team's direction and performance, with its operational environment.

3. Exemplar leader role

Acting as an Exemplar leader involves a disciplined, analytical approach to both task and process issues facing the team. Logic and rational factual thinking – aimed at clarification, simplicity and clearer understanding. It is a monitoring, regulating and stock-taking role, aimed at maintaining focus, sense of purpose and direction – so keeping the team and its performance on track.

In close-quarter mode, the Exemplar may, for example, stop a meeting in mid-flight with the comment: *"Let's stop right there, please. I think we're in danger of losing our way, if we continue with this line of thinking. Let's get back to base one and start again from there."*

The Exemplar's is a leadership role acting primarily in *'left-brain'* thinking. It therefore injects structure, order, sequence, objectivity and clarity into the team's problem analysis, decision-making and selection of courses of action. It is a form of thinking which seeks to strip issues of both unnecessary mental clutter and diversionary emotional 'baggage'.

4. Eccentric leader role

Intellectually and emotionally the opposite of the Exemplar, the Eccentric Leader role functions primarily in right-brain mode. It is the role of the creative, deviant (as opposed to convergent) thinker who stimulates or injects new, different thinking into the group. Creating fresh insights and perspectives and approaching issues from novel, or unorthodox angles are the main contributions of the Eccentric Leader. What Edward DeBono would describe as 'lateral thinkers', Eccentrics are the *natural option generators* of the team. They have little reverence for ideas and practices hallowed by no more than the mere passage of time and the cry – *"we've always done it this way"* is anathema to them.

While they respect *relevant* logic, they are, nevertheless, the 'boundary busters' of conventional wisdom and the mantra *'if it ain't broke, don't fix it'* acts as a legitimate challenge and timely invitation to *start breaking things and re-fixing them,* in order to enhance capabilities and, ultimately, achievement levels.

Acting in close-quarter style, Eccentric Leaders will involve people directly in 'brainstorming' and the use of creative techniques such as 'mind-maps' and 'spider-diagrams', to free up thinking and to challenge conventional stereotypes, in removing mental blocks to progress. The key questions they so frequently ask are – *'why?'* and *'why not?'*. They tend to see most constraints as largely self-inflicted wounds, hence their concern to challenge and change mindsets, in order to move forward and raise the game.

5. Facilitator/follower

This low-key role seems, at times, to be more that of a *follower*, than a leader. In effect, it is 'leadership from behind', with the role-player acting variously as prompt, catalyst, devil's advocate, supporter or facilitator, to influence outputs and outcomes.

Leaders acting in Facilitator/Follower mode reinforce others' relevant contributions that might otherwise be lost, or go unheeded, in the mêlée of a noisy meeting – or if some red-herring is preoccupying the group taking it away from the real business on hand. Typical close-quarter Facilitator/Follower interventions would be: *"Ian, I think it would be worthwhile repeating, more loudly, the point you just made. It struck me as being very important and I don't think everyone heard you."*

"I'd like us to come back to what Sheila said a moment ago and explore it in some detail, before we move on and the matter is lost."

"Allan, please develop that idea for us in more depth. It seems to me it has possibilities that we should look at more closely, bearing in mind what Product Development are planning to do."

Paterson's model is based on the premise that, at *appropriate times,* **all** *of these roles will be needed for a team to operate with optimum effect and that different people – not necessarily the formal leader of the group – will take them.* Generally, experience suggests that the formal group leader will be the predominant taker of the Inward and Outward leader roles, because of their emphasis upon team effectiveness, performance, mobilization and alignment with corporate goals and the operational environment. The Exemplar and Eccentric roles usually appeal to personality 'types' of very differing intellectual and skill preferences – who tend to use somewhat polarized frames of reference – and so are usually performed, in the main, by distinctly different individuals. The Facilitator/ Follower role is often best undertaken, for optimum impact, by perceptive people of high emotional intelligence and *process* sensitivity.

Both in his early work with the RAF and subsequently with the Civil Service, after the war, Paterson concluded that *the absence of any one of the above leadership roles – when needed – was a major contributory factor to poor morale, team dysfunction and inferior performance.*Use of the adapted, Anglicised version of his original model – in both team-building consultancy assignments and within British Ceramic Tile – continues to endorse Paterson's conclusions about the critical importance of the five leadership roles in achieving high performance. The key skill, however, remains one of sufficient awareness and perception, in recognizing which particular role is likely to be most effective, in any given set of circumstances – and fulfilling it. In that respect, everyone in a leader role, it seems, needs to develop the level of acuity and skill necessary to play the role required, at the time, or enable a more appropriately equipped team member to take it over. *It requires a mature – and confident – leader to acknowledge that, as situations change, the leadership role inevitably moves around within the team and passes to the most competent, in the circumstances, to take charge and move the group on.*

Too often, the formal leader may fail to recognize the reality that individual leaders are transient, while leadership remains a constant need. In today's business world, managers have long had to come to terms with the fact that, at many times, their most useful contribution to the team, as a leader, is in the role of servant – not superior, or as enabler – not autocrat. Testosterone alone, generally, has a most unenviable reputation for success and delivery, in leadership, unless it is effectively combined with sufficiently high emotional and cognitive intelligence.

Paterson's model – and those of the previous chapter – all have relevance, as determined by the people and circumstances involved, in all major arenas of leadership. Figure 10 below, offers four dimensions to management and leadership where these constructs have significant contributions to make in mobilizing people for higher productive achievement.

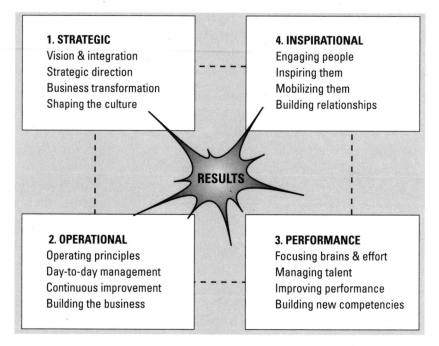

| 1. STRATEGIC
Vision & integration
Strategic direction
Business transformation
Shaping the culture | 4. INSPIRATIONAL
Engaging people
Inspiring them
Mobilizing them
Building relationships |

RESULTS

| 2. OPERATIONAL
Operating principles
Day-to-day management
Continuous improvement
Building the business | 3. PERFORMANCE
Focusing brains & effort
Managing talent
Improving performance
Building new competencies |

FIGURE 10: DIMENSIONS TO MANAGEMENT & LEADERSHIP

All four dimensions to leadership , are involved in creating, developing and sustaining an Achievement Culture within an organization, and each provides arenas and scope for close-quarter

At *strategic* levels of leadership, crystallizing and communicating vision and ensuring buy-in, not by-pass, is an essential part of the longer-term engagement of people. Building the necessary achievement culture is usually a slow, painstaking process often seemingly involving progress of two steps forward and then one step back, in changing mindsets and practices to get to the future, faster than the competition. Jim Collins' findings emphasize the importance of persisting – and not giving up – in order to create a 'flywheel' effect which slowly, but certainly, progressively gains momentum company-wide. Leaders who possess so-called 'helicopter' perception and can see higher and wider than the situation they are currently in, have a head start on their colleagues of more restricted insight and vision in seeing the need to maintain the 'flywheel', once it begins to turn.

In the context of continuous improvement, *operational* leadership, based upon focused, disciplined thinking – and action – is aimed at moving the business forward, day-to-day. This is the sustained tactical influence similarly directed towards turning the flywheel and creating the necessary momentum for sustained growth and increasingly raised performance. It is the leadership – and management – that is essential to keeping mobilized activity aligned and on-track, within agreed parameters and to established or emerging, operating principles, or disciplines.

The third dimension – *performance* leadership – concentrates upon the deployment, management and development of knowledge and talent, in order to maximize individual and team performance. In Jim Collins' terms, this is about getting the right people on the bus, ensuring that they are in the right seats and getting the wrong people off the bus. Performance leadership, at close quarters, involves constructive feedback, coaching, empowering, sponsoring and enabling, to get the best out of people and to create productive synergy, where none may have existed previously.

The final dimension of *inspirational* leadership centres largely on a leader's personal 'chemistry' and professional style. It is understanding what inspirational leaders actually do that is most helpful in developing more effective close-quarter leadership, techniques, 'alchemy' and style. Typically, they:

- Make others feel good about themselves, their contributions and their achievements. They build on others' ideas, rather than attacking or discrediting them.

- Recognize that most people (and especially high performers) know what they want to achieve and so they work with individuals to help them clarify and explore ways of meeting their objectives.

- Empower people and give them the space they need, in order to deliver.

- Ensure that others receive the recognition, praise and rewards that they have earned and don't steal others' kudos for themselves.

- Focus on the 'crime', rather than the 'criminal', when things go wrong, by separating the problem from the person, using coaching – not blame – as their primary response. Their approach is one of – 'It's ok to make mistakes, but learn quickly from them and move on'.

- Ensure that significant achievements are recorded and properly celebrated.

- Demonstrate that they trust their people.

- Be available, whenever they can and *actively* listen to people.

- Inject fun into work, recognizing that, in most walks of life, laughter is one of the best tonics.

Accepting the Nike Company philosophy that, in corporate transformation, there is no finishing line, a critical and permanently ongoing aspect of management is transformational leadership.

Leaders as 're-inventors'

In transforming a company, or even a business unit's performance, leaders necessarily become *re-inventors*, playing key roles in the change and renewal. Taking examples from client companies and examples cited elsewhere, re-inventors challenge the status quo and *create the pressure for transformation*, when they:

1. Confront conventional wisdom, limiting assumptions and current practices by constructive challenge *(ABN AMRO, Hewlett Packard, ABB-Brown Boveri, British Ceramic Tile)*

2. Continually ask 'Why?' and 'Why not?' *(Europ Assistance, NCM, Huck International)*

3. Actively encourage the challenging of superiors and colleagues (*Honda, BP, Ericsson,, Lucent Technology, Imatra Steel*)

4. Regularly challenge the business model (*Astra Zeneca, Novartis, GE – "Destroy your business before others do" – Jack Welch,*)

5. Challenge current 'sacred cows', taboos and values (*McKinsey, Ford, Toyota*)

In making transformation successful, to raise achievements, leader strategies and 'do-how' include:

- Building commitment and trust, through meaningful involvement ('buy-in') (*Wellstream Northsea, Quest, United Vintners and Distillers, Holland and Holland*)

- Making significant things happen, that otherwise would not happen (*Virgin, ING, Nokia, Tesco*)

- Creating environments that intelligently source and build talent and encourage people to excel (*Novartis, ABN AMRO, IBM*)

- Fostering innovation and encouraging risk-taking (*Sony, Ideo, Richer Sounds*)

- Promoting a sense of community and belonging (*Stora Enso, Ideo, Ericsson, Toyota*)

- Inspiring people and making having fun a priority (*Richer Sounds, South Western Airlines, Oticon*)

Close-quarter transformational leadership involves generating, releasing and mobilizing energy – so providing the necessary stimulus and impetus to the 'transformation flywheel'. That stimulus, in turn, needs to be formed by a *compelling vision, clear purpose and challenging achievements*. A lack of the necessary helicopter vision and a communicated sense of direction – that is, an absence of *focused stimulus, from the leader* – creates a vacuum which, during company transformation, is usually filled by anxiety, cynicism, or even passivity and indifference.

Far more so than in static, or stable conditions, during change and transformation, people need to be kept informed and engaged in what is going on, by those leading them. They need to understand exactly why change is necessary, what the intended outcomes are and precisely how and when change will proceed. They need also, to feel that their contributions to intended changes are being actively sought – and valued – by their managers. During periods of change, especially, leadership style and perceived leader competence are critical determinants of the strength of follower commitment to and *active* support for transformation and its intended changes.

As Karen McCormick, Associate Director, HR, GUS says: *"At any time, but especially during transformation, a leader who is not onboard is a major liability."*

Figure 11 illustrates four different styles of transformational leadership, derived from:

1. Helicopter vision of the intended future of the business

2. Degree of goal-directedness

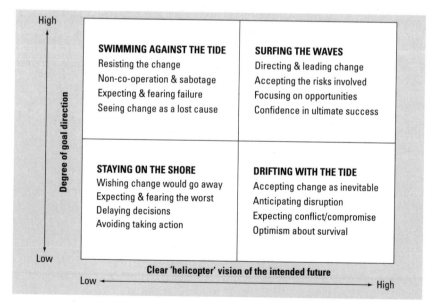

FIGURE 11: TRANSFORMATION AND LEADER STYLE

Clearly, there are many ways of mobilizing energy and talent for change open to managers. Five of them, which are 'classical' leadership arenas are:

1. Open Forum

Invite and encourage ideas and contributions from everyone, but especially those directly involved in the changes, concentrating on why change is essential and the specific outcomes and goals which change is designed to achieve.

2. 'Organic' Transformation

Bring together teams from across functions and the hierarchy, whose interaction and combined activities are critical determinants of the required transformation, to address key organizational and business challenges.

3. Key Players

Key players who are *jointly* responsible for creating, improving or changing a a particular set of conditions, come together, in order to transform the current situation. 'Process' issues, of roles, relationships and responsibilities as, well as task concerns, should be high on the discussion agenda.

4. Complete Team

A complete team, with discrete accountability for specific changes, or improvement, take ownership of the change and manage it, acknowledging that their independent actions have interdependent consequences.

5. Networking and lobbying

Networking is essentially a matter of *discussion and dialogue,* frequently aimed at building up critical support for a new idea, a different way of doing things, or some other intended change. In a study, conducted by London Business School, it was found that highly successful people typically networked up to *four times as much* as those who were markedly less successful in moving projects forward, making new things happen and gaining regular promotion, within their companies.

Dr Patrick Dixon[2] author of the currently prophetic *'Future Wise'*, describes networking as *creating informal 'ideas factories'*. In their excellent book *'The Expertise of the Change Agent'*, Buchanan and Boddy[3] intelligently explore the realpolitick of networking and lobbying, both within and outwith organizations, to defeat resistance, cut through – or, conversely, use – political influences, in order to get done what needs to be done. Professor Carolyn Egri of Simon Fraser University, British Columbia[4] similarly has published extensively in the field of 'political' networking in companies, as an informal leverage process, to both take advantage of – and to short-circuit – the organization hierarchy. To this list of writers and researchers, Gifford Pinchot[5] author of 'Intrapreneuring' adds several interestingly expedient thoughts, in the book's section entitled – 'The Intrapreneur's Ten Commandments', including:

- "Circumvent any orders aimed at stopping your dream."
- "Work underground as long as you can – publicity triggers the corporate immune mechanism."
- "Remember, it's easier to ask for forgiveness, than for permission."

Pinchot realistically balances the radical exhortations with some practical common sense ideas on working intelligently within the political arenas so typical of many organizations:

- "Follow your intuition about the people you choose, and work with only the best."
- "Be true to your goals, but be realistic about the ways to achieve them."
- "Honor (sic) your sponsors."

In Pinchot's terms, an 'Intrapreneur' is someone who applies comparable energy, resolve and expertize to reforming the organization and raising its achievements, *from within*, that an entrepreneur would employ, to achieve success in the external world of the business.

Perhaps the last pieces of practical advice on managing and leading change should come from a Regional Director of the Dutch pharmaceutical company Organon, who stated: *"Find the right people to help you. Find the ones who understand, who care, who can and will..."*

Secondly, from Percy Barnevik, former CEO, ABB – Brown Boveri, who confirms the continuity of change and transformation in organizations: *"Significant restructuring never stops. Perpetual revolution and perpetual re-invention are the reality of business."*

Chapter three references

1. Paterson, T. T. *A Theory of Methectic Organization in Glasgow Unlimited* (Out of print) and proceedings, Management programme, University of Strathclyde, 1967

2. Dixon, P. *Futurewise – Six Faces of Global Change*, Harper Collins, 1998

3. Buchanan, D. & Boddy, D. *The Expertise of the Change Agent*, Prentice-Hall, 1992

4. Egri, C., Simon Fraser, University, British Columbia – proceedings; IMD *"Mobilising People"* Programme, 1995

5. Pinchot, G III, Intrapreneuring, Harper Row, 1985

FOUR
'Buy-in', not by-pass: the rules of engagement

"People need to know who they are, what their job is and whether they will be successful, before you can start working on teamwork, vision and mission"

MARCUS BUCKINGHAM, THE GALLUP ORGANIZATION

A major survey conducted by the Gallup Organisation, in the late 1990's involving over 700,000 respondents, identified lack of engagement of people with their jobs, their managers and with the business, as a critical factor in their motivation and performance.

Marcus Buckingham[1] co-author of *First Break all the Rules*, the book which describes the survey and its findings made the point, at the CIPD 2000 Harrogate Conference, that before managers can hope to build successful teams, they must ensure that their people are first fully engaged in their roles and in the organization. The process of engagement starts with people thoroughly understanding their jobs and exactly what is expected of them. In the UK, Buckingham and his team found that only about one third of respondents claimed that they knew precisely what they were supposed to do to fulfil their roles fully effectively. Even more disturbing, it was found that only about 20% of people believed that they were in the *right* jobs. Accepting Jim Collins' findings, there must then be many 'bus loads' of misfits, with little hope of becoming great organizations, unless management fundamentally re-think their HR strategies and begin to deploy and engage their people more intelligently, in ways which fulfil them.

The leader's role in engaging people and securing 'buy-in'

Experience with the ten companies in our surveys, over a period of five years, suggests that lack of close engagement *is* primarily a leadership issue, and more of an error of omission, rather than one of commission. Managers and professionals of all levels are under considerable and constant pressure to deliver. Information technology – especially electronic mail – designed to improve communication and make life more efficient, is actually having the opposite effect; by overloading people with information and seductively involving them in longer working hours, to clear and respond to their e-mails. A senior executive with a Dutch bank made the point that hitherto clearer boundaries between his working life and home life had all but disappeared, because of unrelenting e-information overload and expectations of rapid replies.

Those directors and managers who are aware of the need to engage their people more closely usually have so many competing 'urgent' demands upon their time and energy that engagement tends to be put on the back burner and therefore remains as something to be *'got round to, eventually'*. Last month's figures, the Board report, due in two days' time and tomorrow's meeting with 'CJ', all fall into the urgent, 'must do' category. Executives' lives are increasingly dominated by the myth of urgency – often to the point where the really fundamental and critical issues are simply ignored or shelved. The dangerous myth is that the shelving is 'only temporary'. Reality, too often, confirms that it is permanent.

Buckingham's *'Hierarchy of Engagement'*, described in figures 12 and 13, below, offers a powerful challenge to managers who ignore the *motiva-*

tional significance of engagement and relegate it to the back burner. Figure 12 depicts the process of engagement as a progressive 'journey' of sensing, learning and integration, which may take place over several months, as the individual begins to feel part of the organization and fully at ease with the uniqueness of its culture.

The next diagram – figure 13 – is also an adaptation of Buckingham's original powerful concept of a 'hierarchy' of engagement. In the latter illustration, especially, the 'close-quarter' implications for those in leadership roles are patently clear. What might be conveniently described as the *rules of engagement* (to borrow a phrase from very different arenas) include:

1. Give far more thought to selection and placement *(Get the right people onboard, in the right roles).*

2. Define the required outcomes of their roles *(Let them sort out the best routes for themselves, wherever possible).*

3. Regularly discuss performance *(Give focused, high quality feedback).*

4. Create enough 'headroom' and 'elbowroom' *(Spell out the 'framework' and the 'freedom').*

5. Play to – and build upon people's strengths *(Continually coach and develop).*

6. Focus most coaching on people's own routes to achieving goals *(Build confidence).*

7. Give praise and recognition for successes – and for good ideas *(Make recognition specific).*

8. Spend most of your time with those who excel *(Get the best out of the best).*

9. Take risks in promoting early *(Take chances with the intelligent, competent, but inexperienced).*

10. Constantly seek ways to enrich and expand jobs *(Increase opportunities for people to excel).*

FIGURE 12: PROGRESSIVE ENGAGEMENT: THE JOURNEY...

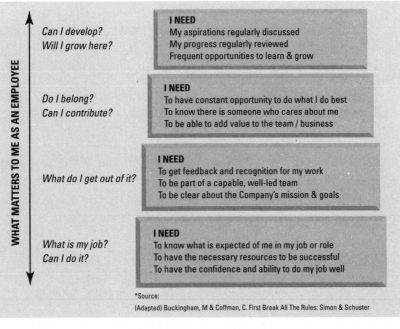

FIGURE 13: THE HIERARCHY OF ENGAGEMENT*

Apart from the frequent failure to engage people fully in their jobs, many managers fail to lead and manage change, in ways which make full use of the talent, energy and goodwill available to them. Before the outset of change, at the exploratory and planning stages, there is often so much coal-face experience, knowledge and awareness that could add signifi-cant value to change programmes – and their outcomes – if only that talent were properly tapped. In British Ceramic Tile, a typical approach aimed at involving available talent and engaging ownership, is to describe a situa-tion – or set of circumstances – which make change necessary and then simply ask – *"In your experience, what do you believe is the best way to tackle it?"* The discussion is then 'shaped', or given necessary direction and focus, as *productive dialogue*, by such questions as:

- *"Is there anything we ought to stop doing?"*
- *"Do you think we need to change anything?"*
- *"What should we be doing differently?"*
- *"If we did that, what is the worst that could happen?"*
- *"What other viable options do we have?"*
- *"If we do go for option 'B', as you recommend, what do we do next?..... And then?"* (which opens up thinking on *three sequential stages* of a proposal – and its implications – and is a fair test of people's capacity to grasp a problem and think through the ramifications of *their* recommended solutions, or actions)

Imminent or inevitable change concentrates the mind more than most aspects of business and, understandably, managers tend to focus even more on issues like – the bottom line, predicted results, economies gener-ally, strategies, systems and structures – and, more covertly, *their personal agenda*. What often become casualties, as potential savings, competitive advantage and value added emerge as the inevitable current 'urgencies' – and managers' personal agenda develop as *personal survival* – are factors like *buy-in, trust, anticipation of anxiety about change, leader credibility and morale.* As strategies for change are progressively implemented and talk gives way to action, managers may tend to distance themselves, even further, from the agenda, concerns, and expectations of their people. Many of the hitherto submerged issues, especially leader credibility, trust and morale, will start to surface as resentment, lack of commitment and varying degrees (and forms) of resistance to change, as figure 14 shows:

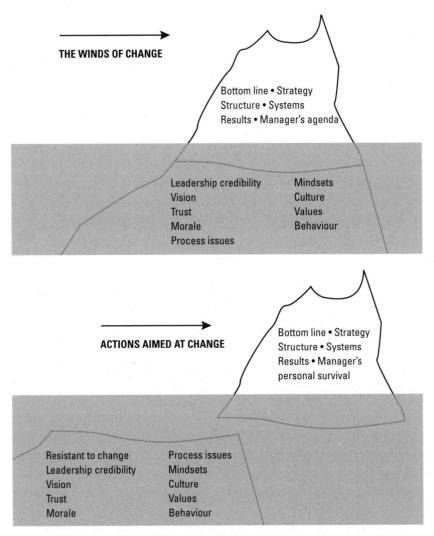

FIGURE 14: THE MANAGEMENT 'ICEBERG' THE DRIFT, UNDER PRESSURES OF CHANGE, IN MANAGERS' FOCUS, ATTENTION AND ACTIVITY.

Much has been written about the management of change and the associated issues of stress, resistance, cynicism and indifference. However, pursuing the theme of essential buy-in, experience with the ten companies in the surveys suggests that *a pattern of highly coordinated and bespoke strategic responses is essential, to ensure engagement in change, across a complete business unit, or company.*

That pattern consists of six inter-related strategies which need to be *introduced sequentially,* but *run, in the main, concurrently.* Those strategies are:

1. Change-leader strategy

Aim: To get the best people into the role of 'Change Drivers'

- Successful organization transformation relies heavily on the presence and performance of the right people in the key driving seats. They are the talented high performers whom people will trust and follow, in times of risk and uncertainty.

- Risks need to be taken by top management in promoting talented people and those of high potential, into critical transformational leader roles.

- There usually needs to be a balance between those regarded as a 'pair of safe hands' and those who are known to possess the vision, drive and brainpower to move change forward according to plan.

The Change-Leader strategy is the critical cornerstone strategy of a major change programme, since it seeks to create the right transformational leadership, from the outset. Generally, it should precede the buy-in strategy.

2. Buy-in strategy

Aim: To build understanding, trust, engagement and credibility

- Prior to intended change, there must be a plan of that change, identifying key milestones and stages

- There must be a 'communication of change' programme, identifying who must be told what and when

- Regular dialogue with key players, especially, needs to create co-ownership of intended change

- Where appropriate, credible external professionals may be used to confirm success in other, comparable organizations from similar change programmes

- Buy-in strategy is critical to the success of a change programme and the time and effort required are all too easily underestimated in many organizations

This is another foundation strategy in transformation, change and engagement. Get it right and the process of mobilizing energy and commitment follows more easily and productively.

3. Knowledge and skill strategy

Aim: To build the knowledge and skills needed for change

- Prior to and during change, managers and others in leadership roles need training to equip them to lead their teams through the changes and to learn how best to facilitate and add value to transformation, both as it proceeds and once established.

- People at all levels may need training, to help them further understand the purpose and intended benefits of change.

The Knowledge and Skill strategy is based upon the need to share understanding and information and to acquire the requisite competencies and confidence to get the most out of proposed changes.

4. Team building strategy

Aim: To create strong teams and to focus team effort and cross-functional synergy on successful timely transformation

- Most achievements in business are the result of team, or inter-team effort. During times of significant organization change, teams may need to re-form their structures, their roles and their functions, as well as re-aligning their focus and direction, in order to fulfil the new demands upon them.

- Team-building workshops and other group learning events create a necessary fresh sense of collectivism and emphasize the crucial value of strengthened mutual support, in new or emerging situations.

- Cross-functional workshops create new opportunities for directed, productive synergy, between teams from different departments, or projects.

Team-building strategy gives new definition and emphasis to the critical importance of effective, engaged teamwork in adding value to changes and taking organization renewal forward.

5. Consolidation

Aim: To review and validate change strategies to date

Management need to review and take stock of their change strategies periodically to ensure that:

i) The original change and transformation goals are still relevant and reflect emerging realities

ii) Strategies underway are moving the organization and its business in the planned, new direction.

- Management must also review progress to identify lost – or further – opportunities for the new strategies to add new value, at any stages, to the corporate (and HR) value chains.

- Monitoring processes and systems must be in place to keep disparate and different functional/pivotal player activities in line with corporate change plans and schedules.

Consolidation strategy is primarily a comprehensive strategic stock take and close monitoring of the transformation process, to ensure that changes are all on track and are being effectively coordinated, across different units and functions.

6. Reward strategy

Aim: To ensure that those people who support, facilitate and further change are appropriately rewarded

- Most reward policies and systems aim to reward people for delivery and results, against specific measures or objectives.

- Some also pay due recognition to effort put into striving for results and so acknowledge the factors outside an individual

- In conditions of planned change, what should be specifically rewarded are ideas and actions that significantly further transformation, add notable value to changes and facilitate the introduction, or pace, of change. In other words, the reward systems need to recognize tangibly those mindsets and behaviours which demonstrably support the change processes.

Reward strategy seeks to recognize and underpin outstanding contributions to the implementation and consolidation of prescribed change, within the organization.

Reward strategy seeks to recognize and underpin outstanding contributions to the implementation and consolidation of prescribed change, within the organization.

Figure 15 illustrates the near-concurrent sequencing and management of the six strategies, in a change programme of major significance, within an organization.

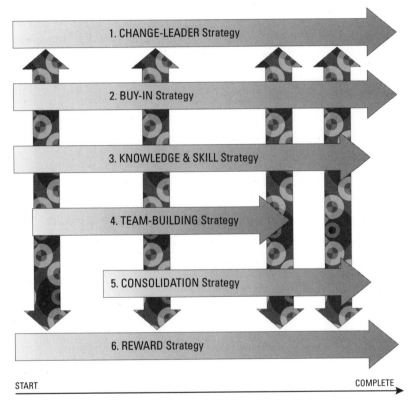

FIGURE 15: SIX COORDINATED STRATEGIC RESPONSES TO IMPLEMENT CHANGE

The co-ordinated and effectively led implementation of the six strategies fulfil the basic criteria for successful organization change (and engagement of those involved):

1. There is a vision of the requisite change which has been talked through and shared with people, by those best equipped to lead the change.

2. The need for change and their roles in it have been confirmed with those involved.

3. The optimum means of implementing change have been thoroughly planned, after objective evaluation of alternative proposals.

4. People are being trained to understand the changes, how to implement, capitalize upon and lead and manage them – individually, as teams and as cross-functional project groups.

5. Positive, constructive attitudes towards change and actions taken to implement it successfully – and with minimum disruption – are rewarded by appropriate, bespoke reward systems.

6. The change strategies and progress of implementation are regularly monitored and reviewed to provide continuous feedback, learning and improvement (including added value) to model the way forward.

Tichy and Devanna[2] liken a major programme of conscious organization change to a staged drama, unfolding, in sequence, over time, i.e.:

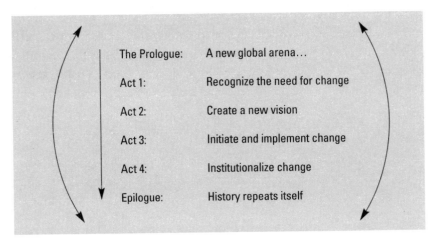

The Prologue:	A new global arena...
Act 1:	Recognize the need for change
Act 2:	Create a new vision
Act 3:	Initiate and implement change
Act 4:	Institutionalize change
Epilogue:	History repeats itself

FIGURE 16

The concept provides an interesting analogy, but experience of the realities of change, in companies, highlights some significant differences between an unfolding drama and significant organization transformation.

In a play, the actors and actresses have thoroughly rehearsed their parts and so understand their roles and what is expected of them. They already know what happens in the future acts – even when they are still performing in act 1.

By contrast, in organization change, people often don't necessarily know what is going to happen *next* – let alone, eventually. Rarely can they be sure about how the end game will be played out – and with what consequences. Generally, there is little or no opportunity for rehearsal and much of the way forward is a combination of optimistic 'adhocery', plans based upon the previous change programme (plus, or minus, 10%!) and/or monitored, but too often piecemeal, empiricism – frequently influenced by a strong wish to preserve the status quo.

It is to minimize just such inadequately informed and Byzantine approaches that the strategic model for managing and leading change – and securing buy-in – shown in figure 15, has been progressively evolved.

A critical feature, in practice, is the *cross-strategy co-ordination, to ensure appropriately timed and continuing alignment and integration,* of the six complementary strategic thrusts.That co-ordination is kept 'live' by regular strategy progress review meetings consisting of 1 or 2 representatives, from each of the six strategic routes and under the chairmanship of a Change Project leader. In most instances, *statutory* agenda items include:

- The current 'quality' of employee (and manager) engagement
- Current reactions and feedback from people ('dipstick' feel for how changes are perceived)
- Where greater value can and should be added to the change programme (continuous improvement)
- Lessons to be learned and acted upon

Ensuring engagement in their roles – and buy-in to a transforming organization – is more than simply putting people in the picture and updating their understanding (although that is a critical start to getting people onboard).

Close-quarter leadership acknowledges that people learn as a result of significant transitions in their lives. They don't learn and grow if they keep doing what they have always tended to do, by remaining within the compass of established norms and practices. Most transitions – be they organizational, or the consequential career changes – are, as Professor Herminea Ibarra[3] states, *multi-dimensional,* involving new mindsets, operating styles, competencies and relationships. Leading people at close quarters involves helping them to think through and begin to address, the implications of such fundamental questions as:

- Who am I and what really matters to me?
- Who and what do I want to become?

- What role do I want in this organization?
- Do I really have what it takes to succeed in such a role?
- Is this what I really want for myself, at this time?

One hallmark of influential leaders is the capacity to articulate situations lucidly and convince people what it is that they need to do, in any given set of circumstances:

1. Differently

2. Now, next – and immediately afterwards

Three critical skills that underpin the clear transmission to others of a leader's perception and insight are:

- High **acuity** and the ability to read the crucial implications and priorities of transitions, as they impact upon the organization, upon teams and individuals. It is the developed ability to articulate simply and clearly – and communicate with resonance – *"This is what is happening...It means this for our business... I believe it will effect you, in the following ways...Let's look at what you have to do..."*

- A strong sense of **anticipation** of where and how situations will change and how, predictably, other people will behave, in given circumstances. In both instances the anticipatory focus will tend to be on *'new practice'*, rather than *'best practice'*.

  Today, we arrive at the future much faster than we did hitherto. Anticipatory competence lies in being able to identify, sooner rather than later, *productive uncertainty*, in the shape of potentially fruitful possibilities and opportunities where likely payoff at least matches the probable inherent risks. The more effective the anticipation, the better the chance of creating informed, intelligent proactive and reactive responses to forestall, pre-empt, prevent or capitalize upon, unfolding events.

- A well-developed **innovative mindset** and the preparedness to experiment with fresh ideas and to explore new options, in order to ensure requisite delivery. The maxim *'Innovate, or die'* is not a misplaced exaggeration in today's highly competitive markets. Resourcefulness and innovation are, *more than ever*, the critical factors in stealing a march on competitors. Indeed, a motto on a ninth century Viking battle-axe saying *'I'll find a way, or I'll make one'*, quoted in Samuel Smiles's[4] book, *Self Help*, reflects something of the age-old reliance upon creative resourcefulness and resilience, in people's efforts to overcome adversity and move forward.

In using these essential skills, in close conjunction with colleagues and team members, the manager moves into *leadership mode*, as John Kotter[5] indicates, when he/she:

1. Initiates, or responds to, the need for necessary transformation and change

2. Sets the appropriate direction for the organization and its business

3. Aligns people with the current and emerging goals of the business

4. Stimulates people's will to excel and succeed

5. Inspires people through *personal impact*, based upon demonstrable competence, professional integrity and clarity of vision

The core leadership challenges in securing committed buy-in and engagement, then become ones of helping people to confirm the *real* person in themselves, going beyond the limited identity of their merely day-to-day *reactive self*. In doing this, the leader is actively stimulating people to access, open up and begin to *use* their creative self and experience the fulfilment of *doing, excelling and achieving*, in conscious, closer engagement with their roles – and their companies' activities and goals.

In fostering that engagement, the leader's role is to ensure regularly that their people:

- Understand what is expected of them, in any role, task, or assignment.
- Have the necessary resources to do what is expected of them.
- Have opportunities to excel and do what they do best, for at least 80% of their time at work.
- Receive feedback on their performance and recognition for a job well done.
- Are shown care and interest in them, as individuals.
- Are actively encouraged to develop and grow, as people, through their work in the organization.

The key experiences of doing, excelling and achieving must, themselves, be derived from the successful exercise of defined competencies, which are clearly described – and understood – in *specific and requisite behavioural terms*. Definitions like *'Be a good team-player'*, or *'Must be an excellent communicator'* are so open to misinterpretation as to be useless as a basis for relating competencies to performance, engagement and expected achievement.

While to some, these ideas may seem semantically loaded, experience from the surveys and client consultancy confirms that this is leadership for real and, moreover, leadership that produces discernible results, by committed, involved people.

It is also possible that there will be people who say:

> *"This is just not for me. This is not the environment in which I can really fulfil myself; this is simply not the company for me."*

Surfacing and confronting the issue of incompatibility, as an objective, positive and exploratory dialogue, can act as a necessary stimulus, or even catharsis, to initiate a long-overdue career move to a more conducive organizational climate and a more fulfilling role.

Arguably, this too is close-quarter leadership for real, especially where the leader is acting in the role of necessary catalyst or mentor at, for example, an individual's career – or domestic – cross-roads.

It is the emotionally intelligent leadership that is capable of triggering insight and crystallizing that quality of learning, within a person, so eloquently described by the French philosopher, Albert Camus, when he said:

> *"In the midst of winter I finally learned that there was within me an invincible summer."*

Chapter four references

1. Buckingham, M. *Proceedings*, CIPD Annual HR Conference, October, 2000

2. Tichy, N. & Devanna, *The Transformational Leader*

3. Ibarra, H. *Proceedings*, MCE 36th Global HR Conference, April, 2004

4. Smiles, S. *Self Help*, Penguin Books, 1986

5. Kotter, J. P. & Heskett, J. L., *Corporate Culture and Performance*, The Free Press, 1992

FIVE
Great leaders develop
more great leaders

*"In a shoal of grey mullet, you only
remember the red ones"*

JAME LEFRIEC, TRESCO, ISLES OF SCILLY

When managers do think about talent, as a critical issue, the ways in which they describe it vary enormously. However, as well as the inevitable multitude of perceptions, there is much common ground, too. Understandably, their definitions home in on such attributes as *intelligence, drive, resilience, decisiveness and ability to handle pressure:* in other words – bright, motivated self-starters who are focused and tough-minded and who bounce back up again, in adversity. Undoubtedly, determining what we really mean by the term 'talent' – and what talent is actually *needed,* can lead to over-refinement of definition and rather too much sterile debate. Yet, against this is the real need, in most organizations, to view talent within a particular context, as a series of reference points and then to define the mindsets and competencies required in specific behavioural terms. As Buckingham and Coffman[1] state: *No matter how carefully you select for experience, brainpower, or willpower, you still end up with a range in performance.*

What do we mean by 'talent'?

In their research with the Gallup Organisation, Buckingham and Coffman identified three distinctive 'talent categories', in which to fit the diverse range of talents that they defined in their study of excellent performance in, quite literally, hundreds of different roles. Beyond knowledge and skills, Gallup saw talents as different phenomena, *in the form of naturally recurring patterns of thought, feeling and behaviour.* These they categorize as:

1. **Striving** talents which reflect an individual's strength of motivation and drive, including, amongst others: *the need to achieve, to win, to excel, or be of service to others.*

2. **Thinking** talents that indicate how people think, how they evaluate the options open to them, how they make decisions *and whether their thinking is structured and disciplined, or whether they prefer the excitement of making up their minds at the last moment.*

3. **Relating** talents which include *– empathy, the ability to initiate and build relationships, high personal and interpersonal awareness, and the ability to stimulate and influence others.*

Similar patterns of *high energy – high engagement behaviour* were identified many years ago by Professor Ed Schein and formed the basis of his *Career Orientations Survey.* This instrument seeks to confirm those needs and drives within an individual that reflect the exercising of particular talents – or 'clusters' of talents, above and beyond specific 'know-how'. Schein identified the following drivers, or 'career anchors', with their closely associated high levels of talent, or *'do-how'*:

Career Anchor	Associated Talents
1. Technical/Functional	Strive for mastery of a role or profession. Concern to excel
2. General Management	Concern to influence and mobilize people to achieve goals

3. Autonomy/Independence	The drive and courage to use freedom and take risks
4. Security/Stability	The capacity to reflect and consider and to establish context
5. Entrepreneurial/Creative	The drive to start something from scratch and see it succeed
6. Service/Dedication to a cause	Dedication to something beyond oneself. Belief in a cause
7. Pure Challenge	The drive to accomplish 'mission impossible'
8. Life Style Fulfilment	The ability to balance a career with private life successfully

Schein's categories provide useful areas in which to confirm, explore and develop relevant talent and reinforce Gallup's identification of, especially, 'striving' talents. However, even the most consistent, thoroughly validated and reliable psychometric instruments currently in use, generate behavioural data that is primarily *relative and indicative – NOT definitive and absolute and talent, as such, is typically defined in pragmatic and functional* terms, based upon situation, context, or role demands. Such instruments are tools – and 'models' of *preferred* behaviours – and just that and, therefore, are simply one means of surfacing insights into why and how we think and act in the ways that we do.

Arising out of the research and studies on which this book is based – and also in the interests of practicality – the terms 'talent' and 'talented' are used to describe those people who do one or both of the following:

- Regularly demonstrate exceptional ability and achievement either over a range of activities and situations, or within specialized and specific fields of expertize.

- Consistently show high competence in areas of activity that strongly suggest transferable, comparable ability in situations where they have yet to be tested and proved to be highly effective, i.e. – potential.

Perspective, situation and context so often are the most practical arbiters of people's performance, in the workaday world of business, where viable alternative scenarios – but not controlled laboratory conditions – are the reality and the norm. In assessments of performance – especially in leadership and management – there is frequently difficulty in isolating the many causal variables that determine, or influence, the outcomes of managers' decisions and actions. Consequently, judgements about managerial performance are, at best, often circumstantial, with undertones of 'if only' alibis or blame, to be laid at others' doors.

Against this, it can also be strongly argued that true talent is the capacity to deliver outstanding performance, *whatever the circumstances, or conditions*. Such an uncompromising view of talent, epitomized on page 82, by Samuel Smiles's redoubtable, self-reliant Viking, emphasizes a refusal to attribute success or failure to 'circumstances', or seek to pass the buck, if things don't go according to plan. The readiness to accept personal responsibility and take accountability should themselves be regarded as essential 'talents' – particularly so in leadership roles. The appropriate interplay of mature courage, accountable 'ownership' and competent self-sufficiency then emerge as a cluster of core competencies that distinguish the leaders who get on and make things happen, from those who don't.

The critical talent that such people possess is that they succeed, because it is *they* who create the circumstances, opportunities and value, where none apparently existed before.

Talented people, then, are those who *consistently deliver outstanding performance, in the key result areas of their roles*. They can be relied upon both to create and to add significant value to whatever they do for the organization and its business. They may be directors, VP's, managers, specialists, technicians, operators, the girl on reception, or the security man on the gate – or whoever.

They are, without doubt, a company's greatest asset and its primary source of competitive advantage. An important study, conducted in the late 1980's by professors Charles Cox and Cary Cooper[2] into the determinants of success of effective top business leaders' found that – *high-flyers who reach the top appear to be very clear about who they are and what they believe in.* The researchers concluded that resilience and the ability both to cope with, and to *learn from*, adversity were crucial strengths of high-flying CEO's. These characteristics, they believe, appear to derive from:

1. **A strong internal locus of control** (They were in control of *themselves* – a critical factor in leadership)

2. **A clear value system** (With clear personal/professional beliefs)

3. **A strong self-image** (They understood and recognized who they were)

} Leading to high self-confidence and self-belief

Cox and Cooper's findings, like so much more recent research, cut across the artificial boundaries of gender, race and age, identifying common, distinguishing behavioural patterns that were the hallmarks of successful high-flying, top-level leaders. Interestingly, they found that acquiring necessary self-reliance, at an early age – for example, being a 'latch-key' child and having to fend for themselves – was a powerful influence on the development of self-confidence and resilience. In adult life, the stimulus of challenges which test and *stretch* (but don't overwhelm) regularly emerged in the research behind this book, as one of the key job factors which trigger critical learning and help to *retain* talented people, within their companies.

Outstanding leaders – particularly those who operate successfully at close quarters – possess high emotional intelligence. Consequently, they 'read' both themselves and other people well, with high empathy and understanding. Added to these strengths of significant intra- and inter-personal awareness, they frequently appear to have *high symbolic talent,* that is, the ability to speak, read and write with great fluency and in ways which resonate with others.

Such talents have been identified as characteristic attributes of highly gifted children by Montgomery and Freeman, et al, within very recent times.

Something of that interpersonal giftedness manifests itself in the ways talented leaders coach – and *communicate learning* (rather than merely 'teach') – their people, including the potential and up-and-coming leaders who report to them.

As Buckingham and Coffman state:

> *"Great managers offer you this advice: focus on each person's strengths and manage around his weaknesses. Don't try to fix the weaknesses. Don't try to perfect each person. Instead, do everything you can to help each person cultivate his talents. Help each person to become more of who he already is."*

Couched in the earthy, direct language of Terry Lunn, former Personnel Director of Joshua Tetley, the same realistic philosophy of learning and development emerges as:

> *"Nothing can be done about a fundamental inherent weakness. Never try to teach the pig to whistle; it wastes your time and annoys the pig."*

Perhaps the simple corollary to these propositions is:

First find the talent – then coach them to become the best.

When leaders' strengths become weaknesses

An issue which has been given recent prominence in both the Harvard Business Review (May, 2004) and Director, the journal of the Institute of Directors, in Britain (June, 2004) is that of the impact of leader talents and strengths which have become weaknesses – often as the result of unforeseen, or previously not experienced pressures.

In their paper Coaching the Alpha Male, HBR, May, 2004, Kate Ludeman and Eddie Erlandson[3] define the regularly encountered subject of their treatise as *"highly intelligent, confident and successful people who are not happy unless they are the top dogs...Natural leaders, they willingly take on levels of responsibility most rational people would find overwhelming... independent and action-oriented, Alphas take extraordinary levels of performance for granted... they think very fast and, as a consequence, don't listen to others who don't communicate in Alpha-speak"*.

These are the managers who have opinions about everything, believe that their insights are unique and right, and so tend to focus on the flaws in others' arguments and decisions. Sounds familiar?

A key factor in the research was that, the more such dynamic, go-getting people achieve and experience the pressures of exercising *senior* executive authority, the more pronounced become their faults and weaknesses. Effective at middle manager level and at *overseeing processes*, they lack the key talents needed *to inspire, mobilize and lead* people. As the researchers found, most organizations are not very successful at developing their talents and channelling the Alphas' potential to help in their transition into more senior, essentially *leadership*, roles.

Experience indicates that there are many such Alpha types around in business (Ludeman and Erlandson suggest that, in the US, the figure could be as high as 70% of senior executives).

Potential is primarily a measure of an individual's capacity to deliver consistently high performance in a different role or job from the one which they currently hold. In a sense, high potential is 'expected', if not always *predictable* talent.

The model, shown in figure 17, below, based upon astronomical terminology, aims to try to identify where the Alphas fit into an overall pattern of potential and how best to help such people become more talented senior leaders.

'COMETS'	**'ALPHAS'**	**'STARS'**
High presence, 'noise' and visibility, but low substance. Not talented enough for the job. Initially plausible, but can't really hack it. Attractive packaging – poor contents. Short life-cycle & removable.	Good up to certain levels. Capable and add value. Potential varies greatly. Egotistical and need much coaching to become good leaders. "Peter Principle"?	The talented people who create and add value. High performers & high potential. They take the business forward and leave important legacies. 'Style', presence & charisma. The 'Winners'.
'BLACK HOLES'	**'UFOs'**	
Add little to the business, or its people. Take and absorb others' energy and give nothing back. 'Prisoners', rather than 'passengers'. "Died at 39 – retire at 65". Need to be 'taken off the bus'. May include very computer-literate 'Nerds', or pseudo-'techies', who have nothing else to offer.	High specific talent and potential, waiting to be recognized or discovered. May be 'Stars' in the shadows. Understated and low key, they let others take the limelight – and the credit. High behind-the-scenes / back-room contribution. Often lack the charisma and presence of more extravert Stars.	

Vertical axis: Organizational Visibility (Low to High)
Horizontal axis: Potential (Low to High)

FIGURE 17

The model is largely self explanatory, but the dimension of 'visibility', of the *north-south* axis is interesting, because it draws attention to the significance of such issues as dominant presence, larger-than-life behaviour, voluble egocentricity and aggressiveness which are sometimes inappropriately associated with competency, or contribution. Many of those who would fit under the label 'Comets', for example, give an initial impression of ability, because they are usually socially confident, fast-talking people, who are both plausible and convincingly optimistic. Theirs is often the 'skilled incompetence' of people who believe that their intelligence will get them through almost any situation. Superficially, they readily fit into business cultures, where 'bullish' good news and regularly expressed confidence, in impending success, are traditionally the order of the day. What they usually lack is talent in depth and competence to the degree necessary, to do their job properly. An appropriate motto for them might be: *"If at first they don't succeed – free-fall parachuting is not for them."* Several of the Alphas encountered by the researchers would certainly fall into the 'Comet' category, but undoubtedly, there are likely to be more potential 'Stars' amongst them – as is implied in the model. To quote Jim Collins again, some Alphas are in the wrong seats on the bus and some shouldn't be on the bus in the first place. Others, as Ludeman and Erlandson found, did have leader potential, but needed long-overdue, focused coaching to make the transition to real leadership roles.

Some examples of so-called Alpha strengths, becoming weaknesses, under the many pressures of roles which are largely focused on leadership, include:

Alpha Attribute	Value to Organization	Risk to Organization
Self-confident and intimidating	Acts decisively; has good intuition	Is closed- minded, dominating
Highly intelligent creative leaps	Sees beyond the obvious; takes	Dismisses or demeans colleagues who disagree with him
Action-oriented	Produces results	Is impatient; resists process changes that might improve results
High performance for self and others	Sets and achieves high goals	Is constantly dissatisfied: fails to appreciate and motivate others

As the result of extensive experience, coaching such people, over many years, Ludeman and Erlandson found the 360° assessment to be an effective 'wake-up call'. Following a detailed exploration of the 360° review, their consequent, highly-focused coaching is based upon the Alpha's typical terms and language – that is, quantitative data which he will respect, presented in a powerfully visual way. As coaches, they demand an unequivocal 'yes', or 'no', in response to their questions *and stop the coaching process, until they receive a clear-cut answer*. A major step in that process is to get the person being coached to admit vulnerability and acknowledge that he needs help and then the coach moves him forward to accepting accountability for his impact on *others'* performance.

Throughout the process, the coaches seek to balance positive and critical feedback and maintain perspective and objectivity on especially crucial issues, by getting to the coachee to confirm what are essentially *recurring patterns* of behaviour. Identifying and exploring patterns of behaviour had far greater learning impact, than did isolated, one-off incidents, which could be rationalized away more easily and their significance denied, as matters to be remedied. Following this sequence and form, coaching has been found to be far more effective, because it was felt by those on the receiving end, to be focused on real issues and it helped them to recognize that they *did* have problems which needed addressing and that *they* – not the coach – had the prime responsibility for putting things right.

Alison Coleman's[4] treatise *Curb your Enthusiasm* (Director, June, 2004), similarly focuses on the theme of leaders' strengths becoming weaknesses under pressure. Her thesis is built upon the use of the predictive validity of the *Hogan Development Survey,* an instrument which suggests that, as stress builds up in people, some of their major strengths begin to change into dysfunctional behaviours and, therefore, counter-productive leadership styles.

Some of the examples quoted by Coleman include:

- The **enthusiastic** become *volatile* and their over-enthusiasm leads to disappointment.

- The **careful** become *over-cautious* and afraid to take risks and make mistakes.

- The **focused** become *passive-aggressive*, refusing to be hurried, ignoring requests from others.

- The **confident** become *arrogant*, refusing to admit mistakes, or listen to advice and feedback.

- The **charming** become *manipulative*, taking unnecessary risks for excitement or gratification.

- The **diligent** become *perfectionists* and over-critical of others, losing touch with reality.

- The **dutiful** become *over-dependent* and incapable of independent thought and action.

This useful 21st century up-date of the significance of the Aristotelian mean in decision making and interpersonal behaviour – especially those of people in leadership roles – serves to remind coaches that most *behaviours range along a notional continuum, as discernible patterns,* rather than simply as a series of *'either – or' traits.* It is in establishing the critical observed patterns – and *likely causes and effects* – of behaviours, that coaches can provide some of the most relevant and powerful feedback and invest coaching with maximum relevance, for those whom they are seeking to develop.

Leaders developing leaders

As Ralph Nader states: *"The function of leadership is to produce more leaders, not more followers."* Leaders developing leaders is one of the core issues in sourcing, growing and managing talent facing companies. More than ever, optimally deployed and effectively-led talent is the real key to competitive advantage and corporate growth. *A successful, highly talented executive team, backed by comparably capable professionals, is without doubt the most critical asset that any organization can have.*

Aside from the bottom-line, the quality of a company's talent management is also a key measure of its responsibility to its people. Franz Landsberger, HR Director (Europe) of Baxter International, a global healthcare company, makes the point that:

> *"Talent management is a mindset. It is a continuous process – not an event."*

Direct experience, as well as research aimed at identifying best practices, appear to confirm four major imperatives, for talent management to work successfully, as a process for developing leaders:

1. Create a winning environment within which to work

- Make yours a company people want to join – and remain with
- Create exciting, challenging jobs, in which people can excel
- Select and develop outstanding leaders

} Build a strong achievement ethic throughout the business

2. Make talent management a critical corporate priority

- Foster a talent management mindset
- Develop the necessary skills to *lead* and manage talent
- Make managers accountable for managing talent

} Develop managers who can coach, mentor, empower and sponsor talent – and deploy it to best advantage

3. **Create the means to identify and select outstanding talent**

- Be clear about what talent you need for the business
- Be able to recognize it when you see it
- Go for it – and get it

} More scarce than ability, is the ability to recognize ability

4. **Engage talent fully – manage it and continue to develop it**

- Promote talented people early and often
- Give feedback, coach and mentor
- Confront – and deal with – retention issues

} Today's high-performers need to be both valued and fully involved

The above four imperatives are the cornerstones of talent management. They are therefore fundamental to close-quarter leadership and especially the leader's responsibility for identifying and developing those who will lead the business tomorrow.

In fulfilling imperative 1 – *Create a winning environment within which to work*, leaders at all levels have both the opportunities and the *responsibility* to:

- Set the example and establish a strong achievement culture within the areas that they control, by defining and maintaining high standards

- Develop and share compelling, but realistic, visions of how they see tomorrow needs to be managed today (remembering that there's often a fine line between vision and hallucination!)

- Create great jobs, which challenge, stretch and enable talented people to excel, finding ways in which to enrich or shape jobs and roles, around peoples' major talents, focusing on:

– What they do well – What they particularly enjoy doing – What tests them and 'lights their rocket'	Develop managers who can coach, mentor, empower and sponsor talent – and deploy it to best advantage

Assignments which involve major savings, increased profit/market share levels, developing a new function or unit, global roles, or improving cross-cultural/cross-functional synergy, are all 'stretch' experiences that allow people to make a significant leadership impact upon the business. Our surveys repeatedly showed that the key challenges on which talented people thrived and developed were:

- Early responsibility, supported by feedback and coaching.
- Opportunities to make a significant contribution to the business, its transformation and its success.

- Exercising leadership and influencing 'upwards', as well as down the line.

- Sharing task synergy with other talented, exciting people who were also high achievers.

- Work which was challenging and fun.

Within the second imperative – *make talent management a corporate priority*, leaders need to assume accountability for developing those who report to them, but especially by:

- Acquiring and using sound techniques of feedback, coaching and mentoring

- Developing and putting into practice the arts of empowering and sponsoring their people

Coaching is aimed at improving performance, *within* a particular career stage, role, or assignment, by helping people to think and act differently – and more effectively. Central to effective coaching that really transforms behaviour, is recognizing that there is a world of difference between knowing something and actually doing what that knowledge confirms should be done. As Prof. Jim Dowd, formerly of IMD and now of Harvard, states: *"the future belongs to the learners – not the knowers"*.

Talent comes in many forms – some of which are not always immediately recognizable, or apparent. Talent, especially leadership talent, once confirmed, is a critical asset to the business, to which value can be constantly and productively added. Coaching, therefore, is a more or less *continuous* process, based upon a good deal of informal – but structured and focused – feedback and dialogue.

Experience of current 'best practice', in several organizations in the surveys, demonstrated the value of so-called 'reverse' and mutual coaching, on issues of leadership style and leader effectiveness. For this to be successful – and fruitful as a learning experience – there needs to be an egalitarian, 'open' climate and the senior leaders involved need to feel confident about accepting negative feedback from the people they manage. Where it works well, it undoubtedly pays off in terms of raising the quality and effectiveness of leadership and management, within an organization.

Developing productive dialogues is fundamental to coaching and building skill in such close-quarter communication is a highly personal matter, based upon a combination of individual style, sensitivity and 'chemistry', as well as technique. However, the right tools and techniques can help significantly in developing style, in focusing awareness and in helping to create the necessary 'alchemy'.

Figure 18 illustrates an approach to developing dialogues based upon high use of *reflective* 'open' questions, while figure 19 shows how 'open' and 'closed' questions can be effectively combined.

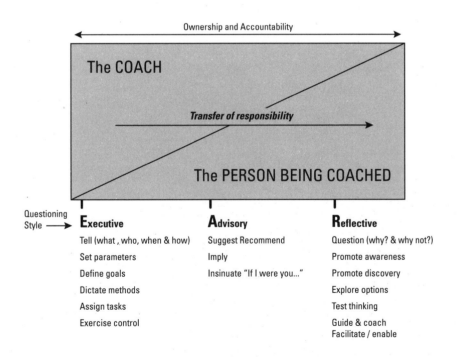

FIGURE 18: THE 'E.A.R.' APPROACH TO COACHING EXPLORING AND PROBING

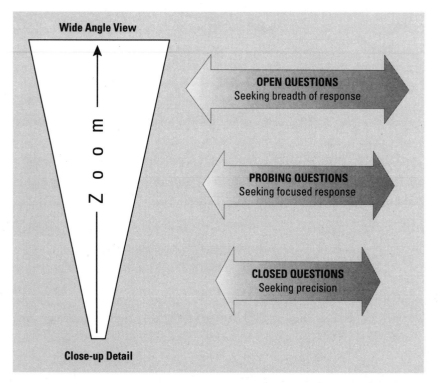

FIGURE 19: EXPLORING AND PROBING

It was Marcel Proust who said:

"The real art of discovery is not to visit new lands, but to see existing ones through new eyes." That is the *art* of coaching. It is aimed at developing *competence, confidence and personal responsibility,* usually within set parameters, which is why 'art' is just as important as technique and skill.

Figure 20 shows the *progression*, in the coaching process, from gaining commitment to, first, goals and then, to the necessary action.

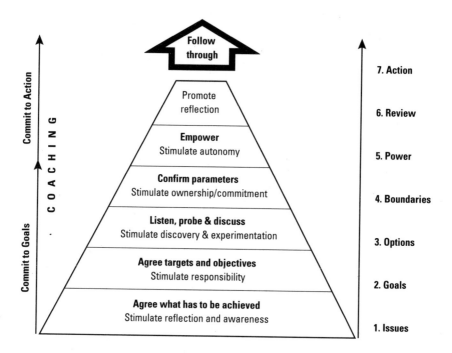

FIGURE 20: COACHING DYNAMICS

A major test of close-quarter leadership will always be the leader's perceived ability to handle differences of opinion and priority, between themselves and others, in both coaching and day-to-day interaction.

One technique is to ensure that there is no confusion and blurring of the boundaries between:

1. **Defining or describing an issue**, in sufficient clear, objective detail to provide an accurate, factual picture.

2. **Interpreting it**, to give meaning purpose or context to it which potentially answers the questions 'why?' and 'why not?'.

3. **Evaluating it**, and adding the judgmental 'colouring matter' that presents it as 'good', 'bad', 'right', 'wrong', and so on.

Mentoring, by contrast, is about helping the whole person to develop and grow, *across*, rather than within the stages of a career. Mentoring creates and draws upon a synthesis of learning, from many diverse sources, over a longer time-scale than coaching

The questioning styles defined in figure 18 and the continuous shift from 'close-up' to 'wide angle' (and vice-versa shown in figure 19 should be used, as appropriate, to influence, enhance and capitalize upon the dynamics of the seven coaching stages illustrated above, in figure 20.

Perhaps too often, it seems, people in discussion – let alone argument – switch directly from *description* to *evaluation* mode, without the necessary *interpretation* of context, purpose, or essential meaning. In coaching, focusing on interpretation is a critical part of the process of stimulating awareness, understanding and responsibility and in promoting exploration of issues. It can so often be triggered and reinforced by the effective use of both open and probing questions.

Another close-quarter coaching technique is that of 'mapping', 'bridging' and 'integrating', as shown in figure 21, which can be used to overcome differences in priority, interpretation and expectations.

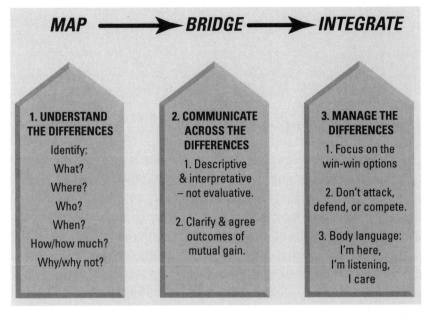

MAP ──────▶ BRIDGE ──────▶ INTEGRATE

1. UNDERSTAND THE DIFFERENCES

Identify:

What?

Where?

Who?

When?

How/how much?

Why/why not?

2. COMMUNICATE ACROSS THE DIFFERENCES

1. Descriptive & interpretative – not evaluative.

2. Clarify & agree outcomes of mutual gain.

3. MANAGE THE DIFFERENCES

1. Focus on the win-win options

2. Don't attack, defend, or compete.

3. Body language: I'm here, I'm listening, I care

FIGURE 21

As the title suggests, 'mapping' is a process of objectively and dispassionately giving definition to the differences that exist between people, so that both (or all) parties understand where the other is coming from, what their agendas are and *why* such differences exist.

'Bridging' involves exploring the differences in depth and confirming exactly what outcomes each wants, by way of satisfactory resolution.

'Managing' the differences is a matter of honest, but sometimes tough negotiation, a degree of mature, intelligent 'give-and-take' and the constant preparedness to see things realistically from the other person's perspective. It is essentially a process of turning competing aims and goals – or even antagonism – into win-win collaboration. At this stage in the process, body language and voice tone are critical, since they add the 'music' and 'dance' to the 'lyrics' and they need to convey engagement and focus, firmness and fairness, assertiveness and responsiveness and approval, or disapproval, as appropriate. Implicitly, if not always explicitly, verbal and non-verbal behaviour need to get the message across, that: *"I'm here; I'm listening to you and I take what you say, seriously."*

Leadership potential

The questions – *Where is this person capable of moving next? What roles could they fulfil successfully, in the longer term? Will they be any good as a leader, as well as a highly talented specialist?* – are typical of those that HR managers and their colleagues have to try to answer daily. Trying to predict success in roles and functions very different from those where an individual is currently delivering outstanding performance is one of the most daunting challenges facing directors and managers. Despite the array of selection techniques available, there will always be, it seems, an element of crystal-ball gazing in selection and placement – especially in promotion to leadership roles.

Considerable research into potential – from diverse sources – that possesses significant congruence and logical reinforcement, does however provide useful, practical clues, albeit indicative, rather than definitive.

The psychologist, R. J. Sternberg[5] writing in *The Handbook of Research and Development of Giftedness and Talent,* identified potential, under the definition of 'giftedness', and around the notion that *continuous self-development* was a characteristic of people of high potential. They appear to build, develop and continually strengthen their ability by:

- Questioning and active curiosity
- Consciously enhancing and expanding their understanding
- Experimenting and undergoing new experiences, as a means of learning
- Breaking new ground and opening up new options and possibilities
- Self-evaluation and consequent conscious improvement in competence

Sternberg's findings clearly endorsed the view (also put forward by psychologists who have studied giftedness in children) that, amongst high-flyers especially, maintaining exceptional capability therefore becomes a largely *regenerative* process.

In a managerial context, this concern for continuous growth confirms the value of dedicated coaching and bespoke development for such talented people. Professor Van Lennep[6] whose conclusions were taken up by such 'blue-chip' companies as Shell, Unilever and Philips, conducted research into managerial and leadership potential, on behalf of the University of Utrecht. Essentially, Van Lennep identified the following as reliable indicators of potential high performance, in roles different from those currently occupied by the subjects:

1. The possession of 'helicopter' vision; that is, the ability to climb out of detail and *see above and beyond* immediate tasks, roles and contribution.

2. The ability to influence upwards effectively.

3. The confidence and ability to grip the situation in a crisis and effectively take command – especially in the absence of more senior or specialist people.

4. The ability to operate competently across different functions or cultures.

5. High innovative resilience and the ability to generate new solutions to problems or challenges.

6. High social awareness and the ability to choose and adopt the right behaviours in situations – particularly where extracting commitment from others is involved.

7. Those who deliver – instead of just talking.

By way of summary – and expanding upon the 'Rules of Engagement', in chapter four – leaders developing leaders for tomorrow, have the professional responsibility and arguably the personal obligation to:

1. Put as much thought, energy and commitment into the selection and placement of leaders, as in their subsequent development *(Get the right people on the bus – and in the right seats)*.

2. Hold frequent quality dialogues on aspirations, expectations and progress: *keep people engaged.*

3. Regularly discuss performance and give *feedback, feedback and – more feedback.*

4. Play to and build upon their strengths; manage around weaknesses and develop, develop, develop.

5. Define the required outcomes of a job – let people find their own pathways to success.

6. Focus most coaching on these pathways, promoting reflection, exploration and discovery.

7. Give adequate 'headroom' and 'elbowroom' *(freedom within a framework)* within jobs: actively encourage them to create and add value wherever they can.

8. Review how the trainee initiates and then builds upon important working relationships, inside and outside the organization.

9. Take risks in promoting and deploying inexperienced, but talented, competent people.

10. Give praise and recognition for work well done and for ideas which move the business forward.

11. Spend most time with and give most prestige to those who excel – they are your greatest asset.

12. Constantly seek ways to enrich jobs and enhance people's contribution – and their experience of work, itself.

13. Remember the value of fun, as a stimulus to engagement and job performance.

The 'Baker's dozen', above, is not an exhaustive wish list, nor is it intended to be a formalized leader's 'charter'. *The thirteen points represent the talent management mindset in action and close-quarter leadership in practice, in getting the best out of the best.* This is not high profile, or heroic leadership. It is, quite simply, a developed style of leadership which is driven by professional care and a concern to engage, use to the full and retain, a company's most important resource – its talented people. For those on the receiving end, it represents a consistency and continuity of necessary *stimulus, direction setting and guidance*, which can be trusted.

Some managers may baulk at the recommendation – *'spend most time with and give most prestige to those who excel'* – and cry *'élitism'*. Certainly, talented high performers *are* an élite, but they are an organization's *élite of competence* and what is being given special recognition here is intellectual distinction, or outstanding ability – not some form of social élitism. Most successful businesses operate as meritocracies and, in such environments, there is nothing so unequal as the equal distribution of recognition and reward, between the outstanding and the poor performers.

The thirteen activities – based upon observation and experience in ten organizations – are offered to the reader in the spirit of exploration, not prescription.

Chapter five references

1. Buckingham, M. & Coffman, C. *First, Break All The Rules,* Simon & Schuster, 2000

2. Cox, C. J. & Cooper, C. L. High Flyers: *An Anatomy of Managerial Success,* Blackwell, 1998

3. Ludeman, K. & Erlandson, E. *Coaching the Alpha Male, Harvard Business Review,* May 2004

4. Coleman, A. *Curb your Enthusiasm,* Director, Vol 57, No. 11, June 2004

5. Sternberg, R. J. in *Handbook of Research and Development of Giftedness and Talent,* Pergamon Press, 1993

6. Van Lennep, D. Professor of Psychology, University of Utrecht, Many papers published, on phenomenology, in the 1950s

SIX
Leading innovation – taking the organization forward

"And on the eighth day, some people in Devon created beauty out of mud"

JAMES WICKES, DIRECTOR, BRITISH CERAMIC TILE LTD., DEVON

What inhibits or stimulates innovation

As with so many factors that determine *how* a company will respond to commercial imperatives and go about its business, pursuing its chosen pathways to success – so the stimulus and inclination to innovate – or not – have both organizational and personal roots. The exercise of choice of response is, itself, frequently more *rationalized* than rational, as fear, anxiety and indecision exert greater influence than objectivity and courage. As Pablo Picasso said – *"Every act of creation is first an act of destruction"*. Such a perception is so often distortedly echoed in companies, under the guise of alleged common sense, as – *'if it ain't broke – don't fix it'*. As a result, so many opportunities to innovate remain unexplored. Jack Welch, the former Chairman of General Electric, regularly took the far more robust and courageous view – *"It's better that we break it, before someone else breaks it for us"*. Perhaps we might add to that thought – "but let's destroy intelligently – and for the right reasons"

The *organizational* influences that have a major impact upon a company's readiness – or not – to innovate are:

1. Organization culture – and the degree to which the company is either traditional, lacking flex and bureaucratic in style, or is responsive, adaptable and exploratory, in the ways in which it conducts its business. Which sub-culture predominates and sets the tone is also a significant determinant of how the business is run, day-to-day. Does the dominant power and influence lie with the corporate mandarins, the entrepreneurs, or the bean-counters? Is the business technology-driven, or is it primarily a sales-led organization? Is the culture predominately risk-averse, or is risk-taking actively and expressly encouraged? What is the nature of the power that is exercised, up and down the line?

2. Organization structure – How much 'slack' is there in the structure? Is it 'open' with high cross-functional interdependence, or is it essentially a series of excluding hierarchies and 'silos', where there is strong vertical control and little lateral interaction? Are the parameters and boundaries of people's roles tightly defined, with high emphasis on compliance and conformity, or is there ample built-in autonomy and scope for initiative and creative experimentation?

Intuit, a US Software Company, has consciously fostered a culture which encourages constant evolutionary change and, at the same time, stimulates *focused* innovation. In so doing, it has, concurrently, developed a high achievement ethic, aimed at attracting and retaining highly talented people. The main characteristics that have progressively shaped Intuit's innovative culture are:

- Constantly change your mindset… learn, change, learn and evolve continuously.
- Achieve sustainable advantage in each business unit.
- Constantly solve customers' problems through collective innovative solutions.

- 'Drive' customer satisfaction through operational rigour and professionalism.
- Become more technology-driven in everything that you do.

Working with the pharmaceutical division of a global chemical company, a variation of Tichy's concept of the 'leadership engine' was used to begin raising the climate of innovation, within the company. The key 'engines' of the business were identified, and the mindsets and competencies to drive them were progressively developed by coaching workshops and supporting training programmes. The conceptual model, evolved in close collaboration with senior executives of the company, is shown in figure 22.

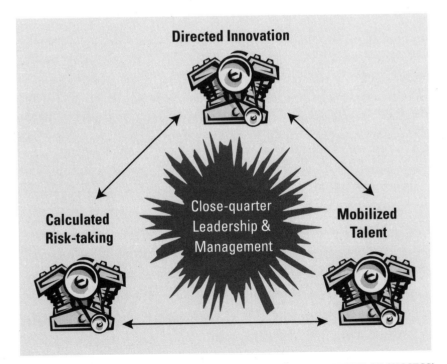

FIGURE 22: THE DRIVE BEHIND THE THREE 'ENGINES OF SUCCESS'

Because of the nature of the business (creating and validating new 'molecules') **Directed Innovation** was established as the 'lead engine'. It was obviously recognized that the right, talented people had to be effectively organized and mobilized, because of the scale of the operation. They, in turn, could only operate successfully and deliver, in a climate of calculated risk-taking – hence the three 'engines' in figure 21.

The key to ensuring that each engine functioned efficiently, and that *all three were pulling together, in the same direction*, as the company needed them to, was effective, well co-ordinated, close-quarter leadership and sound, *strategic* management. Experience showed that the learning curve for managers was both steep and long. Necessarily, the major development effort, over a period of twelve months, was directed towards that learning, involving the CEO and several Board members.

Another example – again from the US – of an organization culture, highly supportive of and dependent upon innovation, is that of IDEO, a major design company, based in Palo Alto, California. Their primary function, as a business, is to produce designs for whatever product a client needs. The key characteristics of their approach to remaining at the forefront of innovation, are:

- Hire only talented people with good ideas.

- Keep out bureaucracy and pursue objectives clearly and systematically

- Make the project 'King' – clearly establish who is Project Manager and what the expected project outcomes are.

- Cross-fertilize in every possible way – multi-disciplinary teams, networking, e-mails, and so on.

- Allow people to fail, within a culture of – 'Try it, fix it, try it again and learn from the experience'.

- Recognize the value of work being fun.

Within such an open, innovative culture, where there is high cross-functional collaboration and synergy, the value that each person adds to the ideas of others is incalculable – as their results appear to show. Implicit in that culture, it would seem, is the daily embodiment of Rosamund and Benjamin Zander's 'Rule number 6':

"Don't take yourself so Goddam seriously: suspending your pride, your fiercely-held opinions, the 'shoulds' and 'musts' in your life, to make your whole self available".

In highly innovative and commercially responsive companies like IDEO and Intuit, not only is the organization culture open and adaptable, the structure, too, is flexible and allows for maximum interaction and synergy when and where they are needed.

Apart from organization culture and structure, individual manager mindsets – especially the fears, prejudices and self-inflicted ignorance of those in pivotal roles – frequently ensure the stifling of innovation in companies. Conversely, it is also the leaders with vision, imagination and courage who initiate the moves to take a business forward into new or uncharted waters.

Figure 23 represents how self-imposed limits on creativity and innovation can vary between individuals and where leadership can significantly raise the levels of resourceful innovation, within an organization.

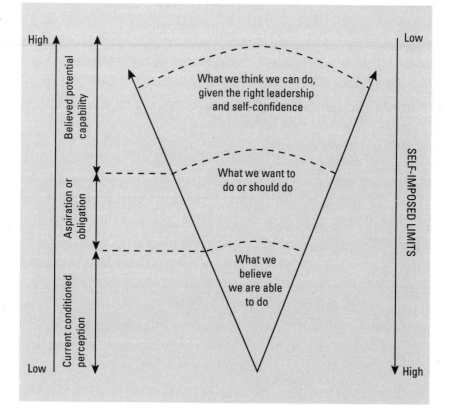

FIGURE 23: INNOVATION – OUR SELF-IMPOSED LIMITS

The implications of the model emphasize the central role of managers and leaders in getting the innovative best out of their people, by investing time in encouragement, direction-setting and coaching.

As Eberhard von Koerber, the former dynamic and visionary Head of ABB, Europe, states:

> *"It's the soft investment that makes us most competitive. It's making use of brains that are 90% under-utilized. People who don't understand this have no access to the solution of our poor competitiveness in Western Europe."*

Stora Enso a major global wood-pulp processing company, whose principal roots are Finno-Swedish, expressly identifies among its requisite competencies for promotion to senior leadership roles, to lead the Company towards its future, the following:

"Encourage and nurture innovation. Adopt an entrepreneurial approach, creating and promoting an environment that challenges the status quo, reinforces curiosity, and which supports and manages experimentation and risk-taking."

S-T-R-E-T-C-H objectives: The stuff of innovation

There are many links between the leader's responsibility for setting direction – at whatever level – and the active progression of focused innovation, within an organization. One such key link are the objectives agreed as essential to the fulfilment of the company's business, especially those that give competitive advantage and/or add significant value. Typically, these may be objectives to find new solutions to old challenges, to open up *new* routes to profit and success and to do or achieve things that have not been done before, or have not succeeded in the past, and are now considered to be worth re-visiting.

Arguably, breaking new ground, pushing through established boundaries and moving into the land of 'I-don't-know' might mean that the normally applied S.M.A.R.T criteria for objectives, may not strictly apply (**S**pecific, **M**easurable, **A**chievable, **R**ealistic & **T**ime-bounded). While much of that old chestnut mnemonic is certainly relevant, even more apposite, perhaps, is the acronym G.R.O.W., to act as a series of yardsticks, against which to measure an objective – and its achievement, i.e.:

G rowth through challenging, stretch targets and goals which focus on enhancement/improvement

R eality, especially congruence and alignment with the key goals and core business of the company

O pportunities and options that confirm, or open up, the scope and potential of the objective

W illpower, strength of commitment and degree of effort necessary to achieve the objective

With, or without an appropriate acronym, the principal criteria and characteristics that signify a major stretch objective, aimed at achieving much needed innovation, include:

- Clarity, transparency and boldness.
- Set well outside 'comfort zones'.
- Consistent with the fundamental purpose and core values of the business.
- Robust enough to be self-sustaining.
- Create value for the business and strong momentum in the right direction.
- Generate exciting discovery and learning, as well as great new outcomes.

The real scope for close-quarter leadership emerges from those yardsticks which mark the objective out as a substantial challenge for the individual charged with achieving the goal.

For example, will pursuing such an objective:

1. Engage their talent and their strengths?
2. Give them something worth striving for?
3. Start their adrenaline flowing?
4. Integrate them closely with the core activities, or progress of the business?
5. Give them opportunities to excel and achieve outstanding results?
6. Provide them with excitement, stimulus and a sense of adventure?
7. Allow them to leave a legacy, or at least some footprints, in their organization?

Almost limitless opportunities for:

- Leader feedback, direction-setting and coaching
- Recognition, kudos and testing learning for the job-holder

Within the challenge of the objectives, scope for innovation may emerge as the result of solving problems by logic, as a result of solutions that emerge through defined opportunities, or through sheer accident or good fortune. It is not simply cognitive style that distinguishes the creative person, but rather the developed capacity to switch flexibly between a *range* of cognitive styles. For example, possessing the ability to think effectively with both sides of the brain by suspending critical judgement, relying on hunch, or sixth sense and intuition ('right-brain' activity) and then applying rigorous, analytical logic ('left-brain' activity) to evaluate the insights of imagination, day-dreaming and intuitive thought.

Psychologist Rhonda Ochse (1) writes:

"The barrier between conscious and unconscious thought is more fluid when cortical arousal is low, e.g. at the edge of sleep, when day-dreaming and in conditions of sensory monotony such as long car journeys, or long walks. Many people are more able and better motivated to use these fluid states, but still need high attention and focus to bring inspiration to fruition."

Imagination and creativity

There are a great many facets to creativity and innovation and especially so within the world of *applied* creativity which is what successful, competitive business is. 'Innovate – or die' is a pertinent mantra in most companies.

Experience and observation seem to confirm six aspects of innovation and creativity that are critical to ultimate success in the market 'space', as it has recently now become. They are:

- FLUENCY – and the volume of new ideas that amount to a *continuous* flow of creativity.

- TIMING – that is the timely launch of new ideas, products and services into the market (getting to tomorrow before the competition does).

- ORIGINALITY – that is the *uniqueness* and *exclusivity* of the innovation.

- UNORTHODOXY – and the *unconventional* nature of the ideas.

- INTUITION – and especially the *quality of insight* behind the innovation.

- DETERMINATION – which is the *resilience* and *will* to push innovation through, in adversity or against tough opposition.

These facets of creativity and innovation are not merely abstract characteristics, pulled out of the air. They evolve and take form, as the result of the applied intellectual competencies, confidence and will to succeed, of the leaders and key players that work within organizations and companies.

Professor Hans Eysenck[2] states in his book – *The Natural History of Creativity* – that a combination of the following are essential to productive creative ability:

1. Lack of inhibition and an openness to new ideas

2. Appropriate knowledge and skill

3. Persistence – the drive to implement creative thought

4. High 'ego strength' – independence of mind necessary to pursue ideas to satisfactory outcomes

Another psychologist, Teresa Amabile (3) writes:

"There appear to be three elements to creativity:

- *High skill and knowledge in the area of creative endeavour*

- *Cognitive style – the ways we approach a problem, challenge, or activity*

- *Motivation – the passion and determination bordering on obsession"*

Perhaps the gaps and overlaps in the various assertions make more sense if we follow the lead of Professor Simon Majaro[4] and his colleagues at Cranfield University who consciously make a distinction between **'creativity'** – which they define as:

"The thinking process that helps us to generate ideas. It can involve – Imagination, insight, intuition, synergy with others"

– and **'innovation'**, which is:

"The application of such ideas, to make, or do, things – better, more efficiently and/or more effectively."

In combination, used intelligently and facilitated by capable leadership, they become the keys to – improvement, transformation, success and growth.

Majaro takes the distinction between creativity and innovation further, in a very clever way when he links them via a screening or filter process. In Tom Paterson's leadership terminology of: **Input – Conversion – Output/outcome** (see page 50) Majaro's concept then looks like this:

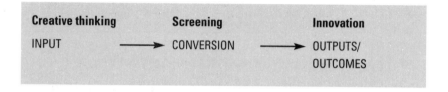

Creative thinking	Screening	Innovation
INPUT	⟶ CONVERSION	⟶ OUTPUTS/ OUTCOMES

As a basis for identifying where intelligent close-quartet leadership can add value to people's creative thinking and efforts, the model synthesizing the complementary and parallel ideas of professors Majaro and Paterson emerges like this:

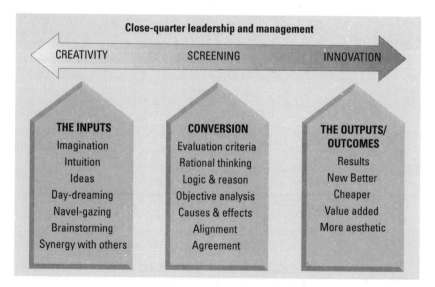

Close-quarter leadership and management

CREATIVITY   SCREENING   INNOVATION

THE INPUTS	CONVERSION	THE OUTPUTS/ OUTCOMES
Imagination	Evaluation criteria	Results
Intuition	Rational thinking	New Better
Ideas	Logic & reason	Cheaper
Day-dreaming	Objective analysis	Value added
Navel-gazing	Causes & effects	More aesthetic
Brainstorming	Alignment	
Synergy with others	Agreement	

FIGURE 24: CLOSE-QUARTER LEADERSHIP & MANAGEMENT

Interpreting Majaro's linkages in this way immediately confirms the potential for effective leadership in:

1. Fostering the climate and generating opportunities for creative thinking and productive synergy to flourish. At close quarters, the leader can variously encourage, energize, facilitate, crystallize and ratify creativity and creative thought, through the medium of:

   - Informal, but focused dialogues

   - 'Brainstorming' sessions

   - Workshops and 'retreats'

   - Continuous improvement meetings

   - Building in short 'free-wheeling', creative thinking sessions into the agenda of other regular meetings

   - Informal, get-together lunch-time meetings, where 'anything goes' and people speak their minds, but where the primary aim is to remove blockages to progress.

As the free-thinking climate becomes progressively embedded – and begins to create a more 'open', exploratory culture – so the quality of awareness, insight, involvement and engagement slowly begins to develop and increase. Greater understanding and a freer exchange of knowledge and learning are, as managers at IDEO and Intuit discovered, some of the likely outcomes of well- led creativity, within an organization.

2. Leadership at the screening phase is largely a matter of 'left-brain' activity, where the disciplines of logic, objective analysis and rational evaluation are paramount. In Paterson's terms, screening is a 'conversion' process, which offers scope for leaders to explore issues of potential enhancement of the company's value chains, their products, services and day-to-day working, as well as alignment of thinking and action, with their teams. It is, too, the phase during which risk and pay-off analysis takes place as part of the critical evaluation process. The more imaginative and 'off-the-wall' the thinking of the group, then the more detailed and

thorough the screening process should be – to substantiate and *validate*, not kill – their creativity. Sir Neville Barnes Wallis, the great English inventor, was once asked where he got all his innovative ideas from… He replied:

"I don't have any ideas – but I do find solutions to problems."

His screening process must have been applied with an awesome degree of logic and thoroughness, approaching forensic rigour.

3. Innovation – the 'outputs and outcomes' stage is essentially about the tangible *results* of creative thinking. The leader's primary contribution will most likely be that of providing the sense of direction, political influence and necessary 'horsepower', to ensure that relevant innovation is pushed through to successful implementation. Organizational know-how, professional 'clout' and, at times, sheer guile, will be some of the competencies needed by the leader, at this stage, to gain a *hearing* – let alone support – for innovative solutions to the company's problems. Dogged persistence, in the face of opposition – and worse, indifference – allied to a passionate belief in the critical value to the business of innovation, will be the essential qualities to move things forward to the action stage. **Sometimes, the most important lesson to be learned in leadership is that reasonableness doesn't always pay**. As Bernard Shaw said: *"Change comes about because of unreasonable people."*

Innovation: Risk – reward correlations

Opportunities to initiate, catalyze or lead innovation and *'resist the usual'*, exist at each level and within every function within an organization. What varies are the scope, scale and potential impact upon the business.

At strategic levels of management and leadership, the risks and rewards are both potentially far greater and usually more long-lasting, than they are within operational orbits – though, inevitably, there *are* exceptions to that rule. The hierarchy of task activity, with its varying implications for leading and managing creativity and innovation, is represented in figure 25.

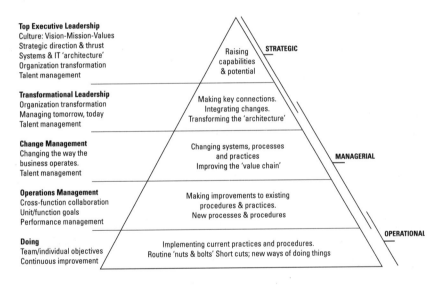

Top Executive Leadership
Culture: Vision-Mission-Values
Strategic direction & thrust
Systems & IT 'architecture'
Organization transformation
Talent management

Raising capabilities & potential — **STRATEGIC**

Transformational Leadership
Organization transformation
Managing tomorrow, today
Talent management

Making key connections.
Integrating changes.
Transforming the 'architecture'

Change Management
Changing the way the business operates.
Talent management

Changing systems, processes and practices
Improving the 'value chain' — **MANAGERIAL**

Operations Management
Cross-function collaboration
Unit/function goals
Performance management

Making improvements to existing procedures & practices.
New processes & procedures

Doing
Team/individual objectives
Continuous improvement

Implementing current practices and procedures.
Routine 'nuts & bolts' Short cuts; new ways of doing things — **OPERATIONAL**

FIGURE 25

People's motivation to be creative and readiness to take on the risks of breaking new ground, are undoubtedly key factors in the speed and extent to which an innovative culture will develop, within any level of the hierarchy of work activity. Guastello, Shissler, Driscoll and Hyde[5] in their paper *Are some cognitive styles more creative than others?*, plotted eight different approaches to creativity, using axes of *Risk-taking and Motivation for Creativity*. Theirs is an elegantly simple taxonomy and their classification of roles has high face validity, as figure 26 shows.

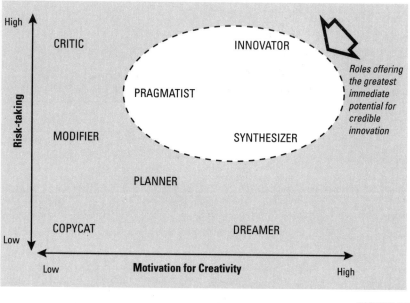

FIGURE 26

The authors describe each of the eight 'types' in clear-cut terms identifying their respective strengths, weaknesses and contributions. Of particular interest are their descriptions of the 'Innovator', the 'Synthesizer' and the 'Pragmatist'.

The **Innovator** likes to go out on a limb with a creative idea and is not really interested in routines or conventional projects. Innovators may invest huge amounts of energy in unusual high-risk enterprizes. Their innovations may succeed spectacularly, or fail dismally.

The **Synthesizer** they see as someone who is usually no more daring than a 'Modifier', but who has a gift for combining diverse ideas in creative NEW ways, which can lead to startling advances.

Implicit in that description is the capacity to create new unities, out of paradox, by reconciling what the less imaginative might view as irreconcilable. The ability to see existing issues through new eyes and to see new possibilities and potential in them, is frequently the key to breakthrough, to creating new value and to moving a group – or a business – forward. The intelligent management of talent, of this kind, is where leaders rightfully earn their money.

The **Pragmatist** is the calculated risk-taker. They are usually prepared to take risks if there is a good chance of success. Often great team-players, Pragmatists make things happen, even if they may lack originality.

There is no definitive and absolute precision in descriptions of human behaviour (one might perhaps add – 'Heaven be praised'). Yet, indicative descriptions, such as those offered by Guastello. et al.- derived from obviously relevant axes – offer a practical paradigm for managers to make sensible assessments about the sorts of creative and innovative strengths that they probably possess, within the teams which they lead. Much of the basis of the assessments that we use to evaluate people's contributions is both empirical and a mixture, of varying proportions, of subjective observation and objective data. Where assessment is predominantly subjective, the quality, relevance and validity of observed evidence are paramount. However, where subjective assessments remain congruent with those of others, who are similarly attempting to evaluate in comparably professional ways, then common sense would argue a case for the *concurrent validity* of such judgements.That, after all, is largely the basis of the currently respected and increasingly used 360° assessment process.

Taking the process of giving recognizable, albeit unscientific, descriptions of behaviours associated with innovative effort a stage further, the link between risk and reward (impact) appears to produce the classifications shown in figure 27. With some licence, the taxonomy of Guastello et al. has been superimposed on the model below, to provide a more meaningful framework for leader interventions.

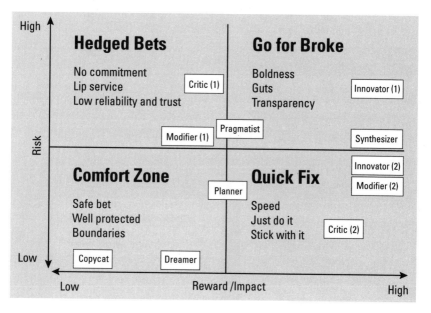

FIGURE 27

Businesses, like Barnes Wallis, are constantly looking for solutions that work. In order to be successful, companies want innovative solutions that:

1. Put them ahead of the competition – preferably giving *sustainable* competitive advantage

2. Both add and *create* value

3. Strengthen the business, its operation and its resources

4. Help them to invent and manage the routes to their future, better

5. Enable them to attract and retain the best talent available

They need, therefore, high-quality, aligned innovation, developed by well-led individuals and teams, capable of producing solutions from the highest levels of directed, creative thinking. In innovation, mediocrity is not an option in today's world. Winning solutions are not the outputs of imaginative dilettantes, or uncreative plagiarists. They *are* the outputs and outcomes of the thinking, dialogues and synergy that come from seemingly ordinary people – and the occasional genius – being stimulated, encouraged and energized by leaders who give them belief in themselves and the opportunities to excel. In the context of innovation, excelling means going beyond 'best practice' into the uncharted areas of *'new practice'*.

Where increased competitiveness and added value are the primary goals, there needs to be evidence of significant innovation – and new practice – in *tactics, strategy, organization and doctrine*. If we fail to invest *actively* in the innovative talents and potential of our people, we run the very real risk of progressively de-skilling them and eroding their confidence – and losing them to competitors.

It is leaders with vision and courage who can overcome people's preoccupation with certainty and conformity, push through the self-imposed limiting boundaries and move the quality of their companies' innovation beyond the mediocre, commonplace and conventional, into new levels of excellence. Uncertainty can rarely be eliminated – but it can be intelligently managed and capitalized upon. That is the job of the leader, going out on a limb, to engage, mobilize and draw upon the talents of those who make up his/her team and to look at the world as it is – not as we would like it to be. As Seamus Heaney, that great Irish poet, so eloquently put it:

> *"...deliberately chose not to bury his head in local sand and, as a consequence, faced the choices and moral challenges of his time with solitude, honesty and rare courage."*

This chapter has, perhaps, more than its fair share of diagrams. However, since creativity and innovation are often fuelled by vision and, therefore, the visual – rather than the auditory – senses, it seemed appropriate to develop the text more graphically, than is perhaps usual.

Diagrams and models are also offered to readers as thought-starters and jumping-off grounds for their own ideas about how creative brain-power and innovative talent might be triggered, managed and led, in *their* companies. Let the final words on managing and leading talent, within an organization, come from Jack Welch:

> *"The best single business lesson I ever learned was to maximize the intellect of the company. You need to gather the knowledge of individuals, share those ideas and celebrate the sharing. That, in the end, is how a company becomes great."*

Chapter six references

1. Ochse, R. In Guastello, S. J. Shissler, J. Driscoll, J. & Hyde, T *Are Some Cognitive Styles More Creative than Others?* In *Journal of Creative Behaviour*, Vol 32, 1998

2. Eysenck, H. J. *Genius:The Natural History of Creativity*, Cambridge University Press, 1995

3. Amabile, T. M., Conti, R., Lazenby, J.& Heron, M. *Assessing the Work Environment for creativity*, in *Academy of Management Journal 39*, 1996

4. Majaro, S. *Proceedings* Senior Management BUPA Conference: *Inventing the Future*, 2002

5. Guastello, S. J., et al, Ibid

SEVEN
Leadership – a matter of mindset

*"I am more afraid of an army of a
hundred sheep, led by a lion, than I am
of a hundred lions led by a sheep"*

TALLEYRAND

'Horsepower, horsepower, horsepower'

In recent years, probably the most frequently chanted estate agent mantra
has been – *'Location, location, location'*, as a way of focusing attention
on the prime importance of this factor, in the selling and buying of
property, in the somewhat capricious UK housing market. In seeking to
find and deploy the right key people in the right roles in business, perhaps
talent scouts will start the cry – *"Horsepower, horsepower, horsepower"*.
This is not a plea for unfettered Darwinism, as the only valid key to selection and promotion, but the primary need in organizations is for people
who can do and who will do, to achieve ever increasingly high standards
of performance. That capability, the confidence and mindset which,
together, deliver outstanding results – *'horsepower'* – develop as the result
of the interplay of so many factors in the education, career progression
and world experience of an individual. Within the totality of so-called
'horsepower' are many 'soft' competencies such as – intellectual
curiosity, emotional intelligence, professional judgement, creativity,

resilience, adaptability and the communications skills that are critical to effective networking and influence.

Horsepower, then, is essentially the mindset *and* capability to make happen, those things that *need* to happen, whatever the circumstances. It is a *sine qua non* for key leadership roles in almost any walk of life, but particularly so in today's business world, where so much of the ability to get things done has its roots in personal style and 'chemistry', as well as in brainpower, business experience and high-energy leadership. Horsepower, in this context, is also the disciplined, *informed* ability to cut through the 'core of mediocrity' and the many 'PPO's' ('Project Prevention Officers') that exist in most organizations. It is, too, the unquenchable inquisitiveness and determined, challenging enquiry that mark out *the low-key, but eloquently insistent and creative abrasion of those who shape and move things by combining strength with guile.*

The recruitment and successful placement of horsepower – especially leadership and 'knowledge-worker' talent – remains a critical issue in most companies. As so many 'wannabe' candidates seek to cover up vital omissions, in experience (and qualifications) and embellish their CV's with more and more outlandish fripperies, so the task of confirming their *real* experience and strengths becomes increasingly important. There is obviously a significant difference – in spirit, as well as in content – between an individual's genuine attempts to develop themselves, by engaging in a range of arguably relevant activities and experiences – and a spurious, or Byzantine, re-invention of oneself, in a CV, aimed at bamboozling the selectors. Some years ago, a major London-based recruitment agency was taken to task by several of its clients for sending them candidates who just did not possess the qualifications and experience that they claimed to have. The agency was shocked by the feedback and acted promptly and responsibly by vetting candidate applications with the utmost rigour, no longer taking CV information at face value, as it had previously tended to do. What emerged from a period of controlled detailed investigation, was that over 30% of qualifications claimed – academic, vocational and professional – were NOT, in fact, possessed by those claiming them.

(How often have *you* been asked, during the selection process, to produce *direct* evidence of your qualifications and experience? Usually, in response to this question, over 90% of people reply -*"never".*)?

However, the ultimate responsibility for making sure that we *do know* our people and have the most realistic and accurate picture of their qualifications, experience, strengths and weaknesses is ours and ours alone, as managers and leaders. Obviously it helps if those putting new candidates forward, as 'probables' and 'possibles' for placement, or promotion, do their homework thoroughly too.

Selection and promotion mismatches happen for many reasons, but typically because:

1. **The selectors are not always clear about which indicators of potential to use, as reliable criteria.** Van Lennep's[1] list, on page 52 is a practical starting point, to which current thinking might add – emotional intelligence, ability to learn, preparedness to take risks, self-starting, the ability to motivate and mobilize others and strategic awareness.

2. **One, or both, of the parties are not sufficiently clear about what is expected of the job-holder, in terms of results and outcomes.** Frequently the questions that seek to clarify such fundamental issues are simply just not asked – and talked through, with sufficient clarity – during selection and placement interviews, as each tries, variously, to impress, influence, persuade, or 'con' the other.

3. **Mutual expectations may be unrealistically high.** A confident, articulate candidate, with an impressive CV, especially one bearing qualifications from prestigious universities and Business Schools, may lead selectors to believe that he/she, automatically possesses the talent, intellectual ability and leadership prowess

– the 'horsepower' – required to do the job. Equally, where the selectors have stage-managed the selection process well and created an impressive sense of occasion, the candidate might reasonably assume that the rest of the organization operates with comparable sophistication and professional smoothness to those of the selection panel.

A major learning curve in selection that is not always given the significance that it merits, is the *transition from non-manager, or specialist, to manager* – where mismatches often do occur. For so many people, this represents a fundamental shift from the known to the confusing, or incomprehensible. Previous highly confident horsepower may be suddenly replaced by ignorance, loss of direction and a sense of functional impotence. In one inadequately prepared career move, it would seem, we have lost a highly talented specialist and gained an incompetent manager and someone who appears quite incapable of acting as a leader. Overnight, a person whom we thought we knew and whose ability we previously rated as 'outstanding', has become an organizational and professional misfit. The *'Star'* has turned into a *'Comet'* – or, at best – a *'Fallen Star'* and, sadly, once again, the *Peter Principle* emerges to haunt us.

The need to recruit high performing leaders is a near-universal challenge that some companies clearly handle far better than others. However, there are still those organization where insufficient thought, preparation and timely induction periods are given to major transitions, in the careers of talented people.

As many professional specialists and key knowledge workers move upwards, or laterally, on their career paths in such companies, they:

1. Discover that promotion frequently means having to become a 'manager' or project team 'leader'.

2. Accept promotion to such positions, with little or no training and development, to cope with the roles of manager or leader. (Often because they tend to view their new role as essentially that of

'senior' specialist – *not as primarily a managerial one* – and no one makes the critical distinction for them.)

3. Paradoxically, tend to rely more and more on their technical or specialist expertize, in order to exert influence and power, instead of pushing hard to develop a managerial and leadership mindset, together with the competencies vital to running a successful team or department.

4. 'Escape' and retreat, somewhat disillusioned, back into the safer, familiar role of 'specialist', whenever they can, so forfeiting their rights and obligation to lead.

5. Fear highly-qualified and talented newcomers, with their state-of-the-art knowledge and tend to ignore, suppress, or compete with them, instead of creatively encouraging, managing and using their leading-edge expertize.

The transition from non-manager, or specialist, to the role of manager and leader – and some of the realities involved in such a career shift – are illustrated in figures 28 and 29, below.

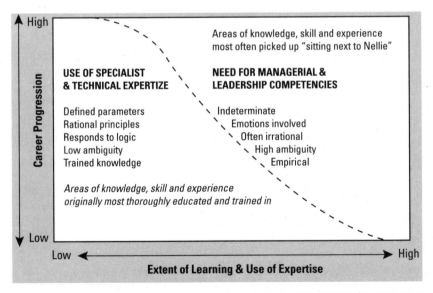

FIGURE 28: THE TRANSITION FROM SPECIALIST TO MANAGER

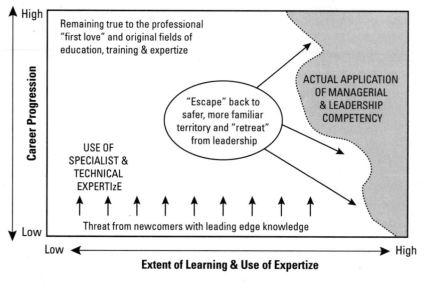

FIGURE 29

Seen through the eyes of the person undergoing the career transition to a new leadership and management role, the following would seem to be key questions that need to be answered (the implications for those acting as coaches are only too obvious):

1. How much relevant training and development – including bespoke coaching – have you received, to prepare you for this career move?

2. How thorough and how long was the post-appointment induction training?

3. How much coaching and specific feedback have you received, in the new role, to help you build your leadership and management skills?

4. How well do your education, training and development, help you to become an effective leader and manager, compare with those designed to equip you to become an effective specialist/ technologist?

5. Typically, how many *days per year* do you spend on being expressly coached, trained and developed to become a high performing leader and manager?

6. What would you like your manager/coach to do differently, to develop you as a leader and manager?

7. What more should YOU do, to develop your leadership and management mindset and skills?

An old adage states – *'There is no personal development, without self-development'*.

Taking that as your start-point, identify up to *five* significant learning experiences – including at least one major stretch job objective, that you will *successfully* complete within twelve months – all aimed at developing a more effective leadership mindset. Where you have access to a good coach, whom you can trust to help you, talk this proposal through with them, draw up your action plan together, specifying the first steps you will take and when you will begin. Establish feedback frequency and review dates, with your coach, for at least three months ahead.

Secure what other critical back-up, coaching and support you will need – both inside and outside the organization. Make a final check and, as a major test of *your* burgeoning leader horsepower, *go – make it happen!*

Developing a *new* leadership mindset

Adults are more likely to act their way into new ways of thinking, than to *think their way into new ways of acting* – which is one of the problems in developing new a new mindset. Learning and understanding – and especially the transmission and sharing of both – are far more critical to the development the leader's mindset than skill or knowledge, alone. Highly effective people are neither entirely born, as such, nor are they 'made'. Reality suggests that they are active continuous learners, who largely develop themselves. A fundamental aspect of that learning is the effective management of information and knowledge and that includes the ability to:

- Access and acquire relevant information and then transform it into *critical* knowledge.

- Add value to that information and knowledge, to increase their relevance and potential for the business.

- Consciously stimulate openness and receptivity to information, knowledge and learning.

- Transfer knowledge and learning, as core, *intrinsic* day-to-day leadership activities.

- Recognize that, ultimately, it is information converted to *applied* knowledge and understanding that gives a business its cutting edge and advantage over the competition.

The all-important need to internalize knowledge, understanding and learning, emphasizes the coaching and mentoring roles of close-quarter leadership in: *(see opposite)*.

1. **Triggering personal reflection and self-awareness**

   - How does this affect you?

   - Why/why not take this course of action?

   - What will the impact of that be?

   - If you were to do that, what is the worst that could happen to you?

2. **Promoting exploration of personal work experience**

   - So, how do you feel about that?

   - What are your biggest concerns?

   - How would you feel, if we were to...?

3. **Stimulating learner initiatives and solutions**

   - What might be a more productive/cost effective way to handle that issue?

   - What are the real options open to you, here?

   - Suppose it did go wrong – what could that cost us?

4. **Awakening the process of discovery**

   - Take a look at how we could best... And let me know your thoughts, by next Monday

   - Talk your ideas through with Tom and Sheila; identify the blocks – and the opportunities...

   - I'd like you to identify and then explore the implications of...

} Close-quarter leader as a 'kick-starter' to learning and under-standing

Managing knowledge and kick-starting learning by reflection, discovery and practical experience, highlights several factors – all of which have significant implications for leaders. Knowledge is not a static resource, but rather one that is forever changing and so needs to be continually up-dated. Knowledge possesses the potential for creating new knowledge, as do myth and fantasy, hence the importance of verifying the accuracy and validity of information and knowledge. It is objective truth and reality that need to built upon – not mythology. Undoubtedly, fantasy and myth play their part in the folklore of an organization , its 'characters' and its fluctuating fortunes, but they need to be acknowledged for what they are. Much of organizational knowledge is culturally dependent, or has a strong 'tribal' flavour, making it a questionable basis for future strategies, decisions and courses of action. Even so, it may remain a political reality and so exerts a powerful influence and pressure to uphold and conform to corporate mythology. In an unpublished paper, Williams and Hodgson state: *"In adopting a truly strategic perspective, the executive is working with a curious double standard. In one way, he is challenging the reality and relevance of taken-for-granted assumptions. In another way, he has to support and even create the myths which feed the corporate identity… The perceptions of the executive really determine the nature of the questions he is able to ask. By stimulating the range and even the audacity of questioning, the perceptual field is opened up."*

The realities of the world in which a business functions are potentially much greater and far richer than the sacred cows, taboos and limiting 'groupthink' of its folklore and mythology. The restrictive stereotypes and negative aspects of myth and fantasy run away with, or consume, rather than productively use, an organization's brainpower, energy and resources. They generate the self-imposed constraints, managerial blindness – and the mindsets of the loser. Even worse, they may inhibit and stifle the talent and potential of the very people the organization can most ill-afford to waste, or lose.

The psychologist Polyani and, later, the researchers Nonaka and Takeuchi[2] made the distinction between what they termed 'Explicit knowledge' and complementary 'Tacit knowledge'. So-called 'explicit knowledge' is primarily the information, knowledge and understanding that has its roots in the formally and informally generated information, transmitted and disseminated by means of the corporate infrastructure of company management information systems, official communication channels and corporate media.

The principal sources of explicit knowledge (and corporate mythology) are the typically formalized and traditional information and knowledge conduits, such as:

- Internal PR
- Company mission and vision statements
- Published corporate philosophy, with explicit and/or implicit values and beliefs
- Declarations of strategic intent, corporate goals – and derived job objectives
- Disseminated Board, Head Office and 'management' briefings

Explicit knowledge is, therefore, essentially the information and knowledge of a *given world* and so tends to be organization-dependent. Its parameters are usually commercial, economic and technical.

By contrast, *tacit* knowledge is the information and derived understanding that is acquired, internalized and either used, or not used, by the individual. It may, or may not, be transmitted to and shared with other individuals, or groups. In its many forms, tacit knowledge represents:

- The outcomes and conclusions of personal reflections and consideration
- The results of personal discrimination
- Objectively and subjectively derived 'mental models' – including those of human kind

- The outcomes of personal reading, asking questions and engaging in dialogues with other people

- Unique learning and 'gut feel', which are rooted in intuition, or emerge creatively as the result of serendipity, 'pristine insights' or imagination

Nonaka and Takeuchi made the point that, if the tacit knowledge that exists in every organization could be surfaced and mobilized then management would really be tapping into and making intelligent use of the enormous knowledge and intellectual power that is right under its nose. Pursuing a complementary line of thinking, at the MCE 36th Annual Global HR Conference, Jagdish Parikh[3] stated that the gap between what we *know* and what we *do* is growing and that there is an increasing need in the business world to convert more knowledge into behaviour. To stimulate, give direction to and mobilize that conversion is a primary responsibility of every leader.

The critical significance of tacit knowledge as intellectual capital, is emphasized in figure 30, below, in its comparison with explicit knowledge:

1. Explicit Knowledge *Organizational knowledge*	2. Tacit Knowledge *Knowledge & understanding generated by personal learning*
Information & knowledge of a 'given world'	Unique exclusive & specialist knowledge
Shared stereotypes and 'groupthink'	Personal and collaborative discovery
Shared universal & objective knowledge Illusory knowledge & 'party line'	Global knowledge Unique intuitive competencies Unique insight and joint exploration
Probability judgements	Original thinking & unique creative ability
Logic & cognition	Intellectual openness, receptivity & autonomy
Organization dependent & specific	Mindset based upon motivated learning
Role-goal dependent learning	

FIGURE 30

The scope for critical context-sensitive distinction, as well as collaborative exploration and experimentation, *as bases for generating new knowledge and fresh perspectives,* within a business, by the effective management of tacit knowledge, is almost limitless. Within that scope, also lies the opportunity to establish more accurately and realistically, what Von Krogh and Roos[4] term the 'scarce knowledge' – which is *knowledge about the lack of critical knowledge,* within an organization. Knowing what we don't know ('conscious incompetence') is therefore crucial to both knowledge acquisition and to knowledge transfer – and, hence the relevance and direction of an organization's learning and renewal.

Much has been written in recent years about knowledge management and its critical importance to an organization's success – or otherwise – has become more widely recognized of late. In the context of close-quarter leadership, the effective management of not just knowledge, but the consequent collective understanding and 'intelligence' that follows, depends upon leader mindsets which *actively acknowledge* that:

- Project team-working, cross-functional endeavour and general stake-holder collaboration.

- Openness and transparency of agenda and intent between the parties involved seems to be essential to effective knowledge transfer and sharing.

- The extent and quality of knowledge receptivity can vary considerably between individuals, according to their personal and professional circumstances and previous knowledge and experience.

- The individual's readiness and willingness to pass on information and/or knowledge which that person regards as an important source of power and, therefore advantage, within the organization.

Emotional intelligence: A cornerstone of the leadership mindset

Much leading edge thinking about leadership effectiveness endorses the view that emotional intelligence, or 'EQ', represents a critical cluster of competencies, without which a leader is likely to be less than successful. Already, several references have been made to emotional intelligence in this book, underlining its centrality in, especially, close-quarter leadership. Pages 18-24 explore some of the implications of EQ in leadership practice and, in this chapter, we explore the concept further and look at its significance in the development of the leader mindset.

In examining the nature and implications of emotional intelligence with clients, the structural model shown in figure 31 was developed and found to be helpful – particularly the analogy with foundations and building blocks.

Emotional "Chemistry"

3. EMOTIONAL COMPETENCE
Inner strength and self-belief
Intuitive adaptive capacity
Ability to envision and shape the future
Sensing potential and seizing opportunity
Transformational competency
Self-control

4. EMOTIONAL SYNERGY
Peak communication and 'flow'
Using constructive conflict
Developing trust with others
Giving and taking honest feedback
Giving respect and due recognition
Interpersonal competency

Emotional "Literacy"

2. EMOTIONAL INTEGRITY
Developing emotional honesty, especially about oneself
Consistency and constancy • Integrity of emotion and intent
Reinforcing authenticity • 'Say-do' credibility
Accountability

1. EMOTIONAL AWARENESS
Awareness of self and of one's feelings
Awareness of – and sensitivity towards – others
Living in the real world and not escaping into fantasy
The courage to be authentic Developing awareness, openness and receptivity

FIGURE 31

Shown as the first stage in the structure of EQ, **Emotional Awareness** might be summed up by the Socratic dictum – *'Know thyself'* – but essentially in terms of feelings and emotions. Stage 2, **Emotional integrity**, comes close in spirit to Shakespeare's exhortation – *"To thine own self be true. Thou then canst not be false to any man"*. Stage 3, **Emotional competence**, is primarily about self-control, self-belief and confidence in one's own ability to cope with life. The fourth stage, **Emotional Synergy**, is primarily about the level of mutual trust and respect forged between oneself and others, as well as the interpersonal competencies which are essential to build strong, mutually supportive and productive relationships between people.

The competencies inherent in Stages 1 and 2 are primarily those of what might be termed **'emotional literacy'**. Implicit in that is a high degree of emotional maturity, and a realistic recognition of much of the cause-and-effect linkages in our own and others' feelings and behaviour. It is this heightened awareness of ourselves and those with whom we interact, together with the *related ability to manage emotions effectively* – both our own and those in our relationships with others, that lies at the heart of emotional intelligence. Emotions send out strong messages about the state of people's 'private worlds' and we need to understand what those signals mean, if we are going to act as effective managers and leaders. For example, a manager under pressure may 'lose it' and go over the top in angrily criticizing, or 'attacking' his people, quite indiscriminately. What may be perceived by those on the receiving end as – *"Bloody 'Hitler's on the warpath again – keep your heads down, folks"* is, in fact, a cry from the heart, saying – *"Help me, for God's sake – I just don't know what the hell to do here"*. The understandable responses of his staff, reacting to the overdose of spleen – and without any attempt to *interpret* the 'bile' in their boss's behaviour – might well be:

"Much more of this and the bastard can kiss my arse", or

"If that's all the thanks I get, then HE can do the damned job himself"

– as, yet again, files are smashed down on the desk, keyboards are viciously pounded and office doors are furiously slammed – all in frustration and impotent rage!

In such circumstances, which are hardly a rarity in business, the emotionally intelligent – whether they be managers or staff – are likely to feel just as 'lost', resentful or frustrated, but they will be better equipped to handle the bad feelings and emotions. It is both in initiating contact and in responding to others' approaches, that they are likely to be more positive, constructive and effective. They will recognize that, while it is impossible change people's personalities – or even 'make' them change their behaviour, it *is* possible to *influence* others' responses, for the better, by modifying their *own* behaviour first.

Stages 3 and 4 – the **'emotional chemistry'** of interpersonal relationships – move us to the the stage of trying to identify just how people make sense of their worlds and what, for example, a particular or current private world, or set of circumstances, may mean to them. As Dr Mike Bagshaw[5] says:

> *"Highly emotionally intelligent people spread good emotions. They get things done, have influence over others, and create an atmosphere of goodwill...This means that people around them also tend to work better."*

In essence, that is exactly what the leader competencies, inherent in the **emotional chemistry** of stages 3 and 4, aim to bring about.

To some, 'emotional intelligence' may simply look like old wine in new bottles. It could, however, be argued that, though it may be a vintage offering, its new 'packaging' and brand image were essential to draw it to people's attention, with fresh, up-dated impact, in today's digitally-driven, hi-tech and increasingly depersonalized world.

Emotional intelligence *can* be developed and since it includes such competency clusters and behaviours as *motivation, personal resilience and conflict resolution*, it would seem sensible to place it high on any leader's agenda for attention and action. This is particularly important since those competencies are key contributors in performance management, self-management, building working relationships, team-development and developing organizations and their cultures.

Percy Barnevik, former Head of ABB Brown-Boveri, underlines the need for leaders who can fully engage intellectually and emotionally, with their people, when he states:

> *"There is a tremendous unused potential in our people. Most organizations ensure that they use only 5 to 10 percent of their abilities at work ... We have to learn how to recognize and employ that untapped ability that each individual brings to work each day."*

The 'Hierarchy of Communication and Interaction', shown in figure 2 (page 16) indicates how much of behaviour, within many organizations, moves only tentatively beyond level 3 and into the potentially rich intellectual and emotional areas of *'contributions of personal uniqueness'*, of levels 4, 5, and 6. Jagdish Parikh[6] similarly urges us to – *"discover the basic human being in ourselves"*, by going beyond our merely 'reactive selves'. It is the fear of failing, or losing – instead of the fulfilment of doing – that is the great inhibitor which bottles up so much tacit knowledge, talent and potential.

As Parikh affirms – *"There is much more to life than work and there is much more to work than work"*. And that is the potential for fun, the joy of excelling and achieving, and the satisfaction of exercising talent in worthwhile enterprize. All rich ground and scope for emotionally intelligent leaders and managers, but even more so where the collective leadership of the organization has consciously set out to create an environment where talent is *fully* engaged.

For example, at Wellstream Northsea, manufacturers of specialized pipes for the oil industry, managers define success as: *"The upward flow of ideas from an involved workforce."*

This shared high achievement ethic, very evident in the company's two manufacturing plants, in Tynemouth and Panama City, Florida, has been built upon four simple cornerstone values, which are strongly internalized in the Company's culture and their approach to customer relations management.

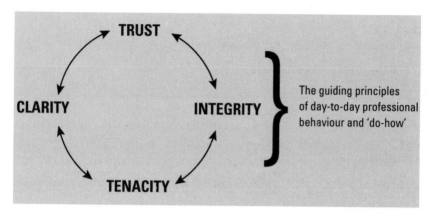

FIGURE 32

The company's high-tech, high quality products – and the strong customer focus, throughout the organization – are both sources of a unifying sense of pride and engagement in the business, which so obviously pervades both plants. From directors down to specialist staff and operators, the four values are taken seriously, as are the three key elements of the company's code of practice to *all* its stake-holders:

- We commit
- We deliver
- There are no excuses

Such is the level of employee engagement and involvement at Wellstream, that an operator will directly approach and tell the appropriate senior manager that the Company's declared code of practice is not being adhered to, if that is the case, especially where responsibility to customers is concerned. Observed leader responses, particularly within the manufacturing areas, have been positive, professional and relevant, with a demonstrable concern to put the situation right.

As businesses rapidly become more global, so the pressure on managers and leaders to function effectively in such multi-cultural arenas, itself becomes more immediate and more personal. Competency in operating successfully across diverse cultures is not built up over night and the learning experiences can be both humiliating and painful. Working in different countries and with different cultures, exposes us to a seemingly infinite variety of values, customs and practices that may be very difficult to reconcile, much less integrate, with those we have been brought up to cherish – but that is what we have to learn to do, as a matter of some urgency.

Most problems occur at the 'boundaries' and those may range from the silo mentalities and parochialism of cross-functional relationships, within the same organization, right through to clashes between national cultures and different creeds. Our planet itself is made up of many different 'worlds', of various kinds and while in business, especially, English has long been the lingua franca, cultures – unlike language – are not necessarily converging. In fact, reality is frequently the opposite, and some cultures remain as differentiated and potentially irreconcilable as they were centuries ago.

Far closer to home, racial prejudice insidiously and hypocritically remains an excluding influence that denies organizations the wealth of talent and richness of diverse experiences, that sanity, intelligence and understanding would ensure *were* available – and adding new value to companies. Synergy has its roots in diversity and there is no doubt that Western rationality and knowledge become richer as sources of creativity, resourcefulness and innovation, when suffused with Eastern intuition and wisdom.

Gender issues, too, if not always surfaced and worked through, may emerge as the result of managerial insensitivity, ignorance and incompetence – with manifest discriminatory unfairness only too obvious, in so many organizations. Even in those businesses that do claim equality of rights, rewards and opportunities, discrimination may still operate, under cover, with 'old boy' (or simply 'lads together') networks functioning to exclude, diminish, or ignore the managerial and leadership contributions and potential of women. In figure 17, on page 92, many of the talented people who are classified as 'UFO's' are women. Some may choose to function in roles less obviously visible than the 'Stars', but others are undoubtedly there, because of discrimination and, therefore, not in jobs more befitting their abilities, potential and the value that they could add to their organizations. Currently, although women account for 45% of the UK workforce, only 30% of managers are women and under 10% serve as directors on the boards of FTSE 100 companies.

These, then, are also some of the issues of the intellectual and emotional transitions that we need, for executive mindsets to be freed from ignorance, prejudice and bigotry and brought into the twenty-first century. For every leader, key questions are:

- What is MY model of humankind?
- Does my model stand close examination, by any objective criteria?
- What is the inappropriate and destructive 'baggage' that I can – and should – dump?
- Where do I need to position myself in the worlds in which I operate and of which I am also a member?

Perhaps in re-shaping and renewing our mindsets, as managers and leaders, the answers to the above four questions set us on the road to follow Fritz Perls's[7] exhortation:

"Lose your mind – and find yourself."

Chapter seven references

1. Van Lennep Ibid

2. Nonaka, I. & Takeuch, H. *The Knowledge-Creating Company: How Japanese Companies Create the Dynamics of Innovation*, Oxford University Press, 1995

3. Parikh, J. *Proceedings*, MCE 36th Global HR Conference, Seville, April 2004

4. Von Krogh, G. & Roos, J. *Managing Knowledge – Perspectives on Co-operation and Competition*, sage, 1996

5. Bagshaw, M. Ibid

6. Parikh, J. Ibid

7. Perls, F. *Gestalt Therapy Verbatim*, (Publisher unknown) 1969

EIGHT
Making it happen – the leader's job

*"We must become the change
we want to see"*

MAHATMA GANDHI

*"…but the foremost of all in the grim gap of
death, will be Kelly, the boy from Killan"*

TRADITIONAL IRISH SONG OF THE '98 REBELLION

The leadership arenas

The leader's time, it seems, is divided between coping with the incon-
sistencies and demands of the here-and-now, creating and sharing visions
that allow people to see exciting potential – and transforming what is
current into what is required. All in all, quite a tall order for someone
whom fashion and that refuge of the fearful, confused and indecisive –
political correctness – decree should not be a hero. In the first arena,
the leader's managerial know-how is called into play as decisions, based
upon reason, rationality and control, are necessarily imposed upon current
or emerging inconsistency, confusion and contradiction. At the other
end of the *'management – leadership continuum'* of thinking and action
– and, now switching into the role of *'leader'* – our non-hero/heroine,

having 'gripped' the situation, re-sets direction and encourages, mobilizes and coaches the people involved. All low key heroism, taken for granted and so often dismissed with self-effacing understatement, such as – *"I was just doing my job"*.

The second arena of thought and action – *creating and sharing visions* – lies at the very heart of leadership. Far more than a mere jumble of hopeful superlatives, a vision must crystallize and grow out of a deep understanding of an organization's:

- Roots, traditions and culture
- Current strategic and operational realities
- Future desired (or required) state – and shape – of the business

} *Requiring the interplay of both leadership and management perspectives and priorities*

In the current Information Age, revisionary competence and the ability to create, communicate and engage people in a vision, of the future of the business, based upon aspiration and ambition – as well as on realism – will remain critical leadership strengths. The centrality of envisioning and setting direction, as core leader competencies, is emphasized by Warren Bennis and Burt Nanus[1] when they state:

> *"If there is a spark of genius in the leadership function at all, it must lie in this transcending ability… To assemble out of the variety of images, signals forecasts and alternatives – a clearly articulated vision of the future that is at once simple, easily understood, clearly desirable and energizing."*

Vision is a quality which allows us to see potential and imagine how this can transform what we do and how we do it, day-to-day. To those ends, vision can provide at least the following:

1. An emotional and moral, as well as intellectual, sense of direction for an organization, its business and its people

2. The opportunity to see, give sharper definition to – and explore – potential

3. Scope to imagine possible alternative transformational goals and strategies

4. The opportunity to synthesize disparate, complementary and even seemingly contradictory facets of the business, by creating *new unity* from previous apparent paradox

5. Serving to crystallize purpose and focus direction, so providing a powerful source of engagement and motivation for people

6. An accurate 'mirror' of contemporary realities and imperatives

Vision in business is much more than an end in itself. It provides necessary context and purpose for the organization's strategies and the endeavours of its people. In times of pressure, uncertainty and change, vision can also serve as a rallying point and the means of re-focusing direction. Particularly is this so when that vision is underpinned with strong shared values. Vision is also a means of defining more coherent routes towards – and pathways through – the uncertainty that represents the future for all businesses.

The leader's third arena – *organizational transformation* – is increasingly viewed as the principle leadership function. As Bennis, Parique and Lessem[2] state, in *Beyond Leadership*:

> "The new paradigm manager is primarily acting in the role of transformational leader."

In such a role, the leader is acting variously as explorer, catalyst and enabler. Currently, so many businesses are experiencing dramatic re-mapping and restructuring of traditional organizational boundaries, as people struggle to define, act out and fulfil new roles and engage in new partnerships and work relationships. Disappearing previous clarity of role and contribution concentrates minds on self-preservation, protection of territory and the power-play of life-or-death organizational survival. Transforming an organization – with its visionary connotations of aspiration, major change and thus risk – but without any requirement for heroism, sounds like a contradiction in terms. Without courage, other critical change-agent skills will not be enough to effect and sustain transformation through the inevitable, successive 'political' battles. Leaders responsible for transforming an organization, by definition, embark on an heroic journey. What is more – *it is a path without end, where many of the staging-posts and destinations are indeterminate.* Hardly stuff for the faint-hearted!

In more politically-driven organizations, where the interplay of people, power and politics becomes the major determinant of role boundaries, status and authority, leaders may be forced to act as what Tom Cummings[3] describes as a *'facipulator'*, as they work at finding the realistic answers to questions such as:

1. Who is now in charge of what and whom are they in charge of ?

2. Who now is responsible for doing what – and in which circumstances?

3. Who, precisely, are 'we' and who is/isn't part of 'us'?

4. Where does the accountability lie, for this and for that?

5. So, what's in this for me and for us?

Some of the realities of transformation which leaders may need to sort out, if organizational change is to work

As 'facipulators', enablers and change-agents, leaders may have to confront and deal quickly and firmly with a range of counter-productive behaviours and dysfunctional 'boundaries', during transformation and transition, including:

- New, often assumed, territorial 'rights' and imperatives
- New, often assumed and potentially destructive authority

} *Problems which become even more complex and exaggerated in 'virtual' organizations and dispersed structures*

Leaders as net-workers

The successive, changing and adaptive networks of people, that increasingly characterize the ways in which companies operate, emphasize the *directing*, as well as enabling, roles of leaders. Their task, so often, is to establish necessary degrees of autonomy and independence, but within clear frameworks of *interdependence* and mutual support.

The increasing shift from 'corporation' to *enterprize*, represents a fundamental transition in the life-cycles of most businesses, where the functional operating norm becomes one of – *freedom within a framework*. Key tasks for leaders then become those of appointing, in turn, leaders who:

1. Are capable of taking professional ownership and responsibility for their own work domain and its outputs, that is – they are well able to run their own business unit.

2. Have high competency in mediating between their function and other comparably, empowered and autonomous units.

Success in the more 'organic' forms of collaboration and partnering, that are increasingly needed in organizations, depends to a large degree upon the 'networking' skills of the leaders and other key players. Professor Shoshana Zuboff[4] defines 'networking' as: *"the gaining of necessary goodwill from others to support people, tasks or projects, by oral communication."*

As Roy Sheppard[5] suggests, good net-workers – as opposed to 'party pests' – tend to create and become part of 'virtuous circles', where they both give out and receive help and, in so doing, *continue* to build on their contacts. Networks are, in effect, 'ideas factories' where continuous improvement, the adding of value and the strengthening of critical relationships all become possible in informal, yet very powerful ways. Both networking, capable of generating productive synergy – and the successful management of such collaborative networks – are increasingly emerging as critical leadership competencies.

Knowledge most certainly is power – hence people's concern to retain it as much as they can. Networking must accept that dictum, but the process – well-managed and led – rapidly demonstrates the far greater power of *shared* knowledge and the value that can be added to both individual and collective effort – on the basis that – *'Alone, I can walk, but together – WE can fly'.*

In addition to generating frequently much needed goodwill and support, effective net-working creates opportunities for:

- Collaborative sounding boards to explore any number of challenges, concerns and ideas.

- What Zuboff terms 'informating' – and keeping one another updated and 'in the loop', as a matter of course, through the informal medium of 'listening posts'.

- Increasing engagement and congruent alignment between different individuals, functions, projects and business units.

- 'Match-making' and connectivity between key players who would normally 'lose out', by not making contact with each other.

- Generating necessary 'peak communication' between people (see figure 2, page 16) to stimulate focused synergy and productive creativity.

- Strengthening 'centrality' and influence within the organization – yet remaining realistically aware of the potential downside of networking, once it comes to be seen as manipulative 'politicking', with a consequent loss of trust.

- The creation of a culture, throughout the organization, of *co-operative self-sufficiency*, where mature self-reliance alternates, as appropriate, with mutual support and necessary collaborative joint working.

Managers are operating as leaders in a world characterized by increasing complexity and paradox, less certainty, but almost limitless choice and opportunity. Hand in hand with most opportunity, however, goes risk and particularly so in the areas of indeterminate opportunity that represent *productive uncertainty* for an enterprize. In such conditions, especially, managing risk and opportunity usually means that the opportunities – and the potential advantages that they may offer – frequently:

- Arrive suddenly and unexpectedly – necessitating rapid, decisive and courageous action.

- Occur haphazardly, randomly or fortuitously, with no logic, sequence, or discernible pattern.

- Surface in 'disguise', so that they are not immediately recognizable for what they truly are.

- Emerge as a unique or transitional aberration, which catches people unprepared, or off-guard.

- Involve considerable change, 'pain', or hassle.

Leading the way to tomorrow

Managing the present, in order to create and shape the organization's future, with its challenges of risk and potential payoff, involves the complementary tasks of managing the business, day-to-day and managing people's performance and potential.

Managing today, to get to the desired tomorrow, therefore means:

1. Ensuring the continuous, monitored and focused transformation of the business

2. Regular, informed environmental scanning, scenario building, evaluation and adaptive re-building

3. Constantly making sense of and imposing coherence and order upon the tenuous links between opportunism, serendipity and uncertainty, in order to 'read' the future, based upon the best available intelligence

4. Taking major decisions about the direction, shape, positioning and profitability of the organization – usually on the basis of imperfect information and knowledge

5. Constantly relating and re-aligning the organization to the changing – often contradictory – imperatives of its wider, strategic environment

6. Fulfilling all of the above, while maintaining profit levels and competitive advantage – and remembering to be, first and foremost, a close-quarter leader to the team and its members.

And we don't need heroes for leaders...?

Being a 'hero', or 'heroine', in the context of close-quarter leadership, as defined here, is NOT about kudos-grabbing egotism, or being a testosterone-driven superhuman. Heroic behaviour is essentially that of someone who has the courage and personal resilience to:

- Take tough, unpalatable decisions when they need to be taken

- See a daunting task or testing assignment right through, from start to completion

- Holds by beliefs and values that are morally right, but don't match the often spurious criteria of fad, whim, or prevailing political correctness

- Face up to clashes between truth and personal loyalty and stick to their chosen path, despite strong disapproval, or even rejection, from superiors and colleagues.

- Live with the reality that it is ethically sound to take a tough line with people, in order to move them – or the organization – forward, in the right direction, for the success of the business.

- Have the humility and be big enough to say – "I got it wrong: we should do it your way"

- Live the adage – 'Must do it – so, just do it'.

Understated heroism, apart from low-key courage and quiet, indestructible persistence, is essentially selfless and devoted to the growth and success of others – or to causes beyond the self. It is to be found in the roles of those who serve, facilitate, enable and catalyze, just as much as among those who lead from the front. Frequently paired with such self-effacing courage, is a generosity of spirit which forgives without condoning, but which, nevertheless upholds standards and ideals. Necessary 'cutting-edge' is demonstrated professionally – while showing respect for others – in the spirit of Edmund Burke's statement:

"There comes a time, when forbearance ceases to be a virtue."

Heroic journeys and the related, team-orientated leader styles which work, don't always sit easily with the mindsets of those traditional managers who work principally by the rules and obligations of hierarchical propriety. When managerial behaviour tends to be an emotional roller-coaster of deferential dips, alternating with macho, polemic peaks, there is little hope of intelligent, sensitive close-quarter leadership, with its consequent productive creativity, and a committed spirit of experimentation and transformation.

As Professor Tom Cannon[6] affirms:

> " Collaboration is more important than control" and "Performance is more important than deference."

Today, there are more graduates and qualified people, who are better informed and less accepting, than those of previous generations. Socially, we are living in a more egalitarian age, where former, traditional 'badges' of status and rank are being replaced by respect for professional competence and the 'street cred' of do-how and delivery. As a consequence, people expect to be led by capable, trustworthy and consistent leaders who value, respect and know how to release and use their knowledge and skill in challenging, worthwhile enterprize.

People working in organizations engage in the business, collaborate, and give of their best, when they have confidence in leaders who demonstrably value their efforts and achievements by *actions* – as well as the 'right' words. Especially in times of high pressure and change, winning hearts and minds is a matter of credibility, trust and mutual respect – those remain the eternal imperatives of leadership.

Perhaps never before, in business, have the leadership competencies of managers been so critically put to the test and evaluated, as they are in today's Information Age.

Who have I learned – and continue to learn – from, about being a leader?

Who are the people, in your life, to date, who have had the greatest influence on your development and career progression, as a leader? Think about those – from ALL walks of life – who have made the greatest impact on you, *shaping your thinking and actions*, in the continuing development of your leadership and management styles. Think especially, of those people whose example, or guidance, have helped you to grow significantly as a person and as a leader

Imagine yourself as a Managing Director, with each of the people whom you have selected, sitting in front of you, around an imaginary boardroom table, reinforcing the messages they have given you, as shown in figure 33. Choose the people who will form your *'Leadership Board of Directors'*. Include both positive and negative contacts from whom you have acquired critical learning, about leading and managing people. Usually, somewhere between twelve and twenty such sources are sufficient.

Identify each 'Director' who is 'seated' around your table and summarize, in a few words, the key messages about leadership that you picked up from them. Ideally, one or two sentences should be enough to crystallize the learning that you gained from each one. On the boardroom 'table top', summarize, as succinctly as possible – those key learning points and 'life messages' that you have picked up yourself, from your day-to-day experiences, including the *collective* impact of your chosen 'directors'. Your 'life messages' should help to crystallize your leadership mindset.

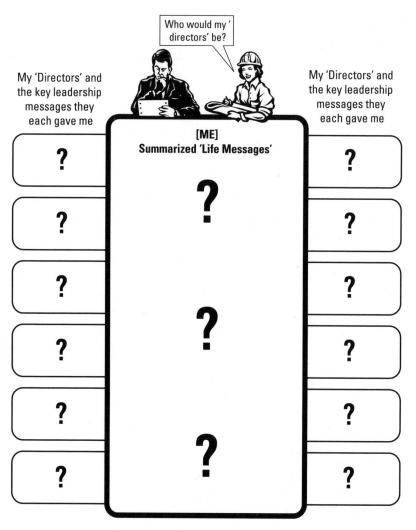

My 'Directors' and the key leadership messages they each gave me

Who would my 'directors' be?

[ME]
Summarized 'Life Messages'

My 'Directors' and the key leadership messages they each gave me

FIGURE 33
Source: (adapted and updated) Michael Williams, **The War for Talent***, London, CIPD: 2000*

When you have completed your 'Personal Board of Directors' – including your summarized 'life messages' – look for compatibility, reinforcement and any contradictions, in the two sets of messages *(Directors' key points and the life messages you have acquired, through personal experience).*

Talk through the implications of these two sources of learning with someone whom you could trust as a competent mentor. Some questions that might be helpful to explore with your mentor are:

1. Do any of these messages represent 'baggage' which you now ought to get rid of?

2. Is it time for some fresh, new 'Directors', with different messages?

3. Who, specifically – and why? – would you like to see sitting at your boardroom table?

4. Whose personal 'Board of Directors' would you like to be invited to sit on? Why?

5. What will you now do differently – and make greater use of – these sources of learning?

Simply as a source of ideas, figure 34 is offered as a 'live' example of a 'Board of Directors', which is updated annually. The original has sixteen 'directors' and four are omitted, because of lack of space here.

My 'Directors' and the key leadership messages they each gave me	**[ME]** **Summarized 'Life Messages'**	My 'Directors' and the key leadership messages they each gave me
Wife, Brenda *Don't judge – there's always another side to a story.* *Be loyal, be loving, be kind*	It's really up to me – no one owes me a living	Daughter, Susie Life is for real – live it. Don't compromise on standards *Blood is thicker than water*
	Live life – you get out of it what you put in to it	
Son, Jonathan Egalitarianism. Balance and perspective. *Tolerance.* *"You can always look at it this way!"*	Don't waste time, talent and effort Focus on the 'crime' – not the 'criminal' We'll find a way – or we'll make one	Grandfather, from Tipperary Be caring and gentle. Never be cruel. *There is so much to life – so look for it*
Mother It's ok to have fun and to laugh at yourself. *Live life each day at a time*	You're only as good as your *next* job Bite the bullet and go for it! Quality and professionalism are the "musts"	Father *If a job's worth doing – it's worth doing properly.* A love of things Celtic and Gaelic
Troop Commander, Don. Never give in – go that extra step. *It's ok to take tough decisions.* *Go for it!*	You never, never stop learning (if you do – you're dead) Adapt and innovate they're a key to success - try looking at things *differently* (it won't hurt you!)	School bully, Geoffrey *Fight back and always fight to win.* *Never tolerate injustice, or bullying*
Russian teacher Colonel Yevgenny Galko. *Don't just talk about it –* *go there! Do it and get it right*	Hard and tough are ok – harsh and unjust are unacceptable It's ok to ask for help – TEAMWORK wins!	IMD Colleague, Anne *Don't start stopping and don't stop starting.* *People grow old by deserting their ideals*
Friend, Roy *Try new things.* *Experiment. Innovate.* *Be resourceful and adaptable. Enthusiasm!*	In a bad situation, a sense of humour is a great asset. Laughter is one of the best medicines Be polite, stay calm and hit very hard	Boss, Dennis Sensitivity to and awareness of others. Listen to people. Ask 'why?' and 'why not?'

FIGURE 34

Source: (adapted and updated) Michael Williams, **The War for Talent***, London, CIPD: 2000*

The exercise described in the preceding pages and in figures 33 and 34, represents a personal and professional 'stock-take' and, therefore, an opportunity for self-reflection about one's own approach to leadership. As a personal review, it begs several questions about the quality, direction and state of an individual's learning, leader style, development of competencies – and career progression. It can reflect, too, the evolving nature of the business and its changing requirements for leadership. Essentially, it is offered here as a tool for both structured self-development and mentoring – and as a *different* way of identifying the 'plusses' and 'minuses' of an individual's leadership abilities and mindset.

Such a focused and individual stock-take acts as an intellectual, emotional and moral 'Global Positioning System' (GPS) against which to check judgements and decisions, made day-to-day, in the context of major personal beliefs and values. With its somewhat unforgiving criteria, it offers a more action-orientated basis for self-management and self-development than do many tools and techniques. While its focus is primarily upon an individual's strengths, signals indicating weaknesses are also to be found there, as a powerful reminder and personal 'early warning system'.

The crystallized messages represent, with practised interpretation, much of what a person transparently stands for as a leader and as a human being, how they connect and engage with the world around them and what they passionately believe in. *The leader's role is, first and foremost, a selfless one and the more engaged the leader, the greater need for capability, availability and commitment.*

Exploring the results of the stock-take should give important clues for a person's continuing growth and development, in at least the following areas of leadership and management and how they are likely to:

- Develop and apply their particular model of human kind
- Attract – or, otherwise – and interact with other people
- Relate to and engage with people from other cultures
- Function under pressure (and indicate what *they* probably regard as dysfunctional 'pressure')
- Be motivated and what, especially, will most likely light their particular rocket

- Operate at their most consistently capable and in which conditions, or environments

- Respond, themselves, to others' different styles of leadership and management

More than previously, organizations need to be very clear about how capable each of their managers is, especially in the role of a leader. In a world where adaptive competency represents a more appropriate mindset, than one governed by conventional wisdom, managers themselves need to be crystal clear about how they measure up as leaders, capable of moving their businesses forward through the efforts of their people. Where we see real success today, usually somebody, assuming a leadership role, acted with courage as well as with competence and conviction. *In essence, leadership by example.*

Constantly added value and competitive advantage, the cornerstones of organizations' survival, are ensured by competently managed and courageously led, empowered and talented people. Moreover, they are people whose talents are continually developed and further enhanced, by being *intelligently* deployed for maximum effect. Getting the very best out of people – and ensuring that *they*, in turn, receive the best possible opportunities for professional challenge and personal growth – is what close-quarter leadership is really about. Close-quarter leadership is neither fad nor fetish. It isn't put forward here, as current 'flavour' or fashion , but rather as an observed *evolving body of applied awareness, understanding and competencies clusters*, adaptable to the individual flair, unique styles and personal skills of the practitioners. At its core, are mindsets, in a continuous state of learning, constantly searching for, exploring – and committing to – ever better ways to lead, mobilize and develop people.

Chapter eight references

1. Bennis, W. & Nanus, B. *Leaders* Harper & Row, 1985

2. Bennis, W., Parikh, J. & Lessem, R. *Beyond Leadership,* Blackwell, 1994

3. Cummings, T. *Proceedings,* BUPA Conference, *Inventing the Future,* 2002

4. Zuboff, S. *In the Age of the Smart Machine,* Heinemann, 1988

5. Sheppard, R. *Standing Out from the Crowd,* Director, January 1998

6. Cannon, T., in Watts, S. *Career Directors have a Charter to Learn How to do their Job,* Sunday Telegraph,18 July, 1999

Other titles from Thorogood

THE A-Z OF EMPLOYMENT PRACTICE

David Martin

£19.99 paperback, £42.00 hardback

Published November 2004

This book provides comprehensive, practical guidance on personnel law and practice at a time when employers are faced with a maze of legislation, obligations and potential penalties. It provides detailed and practical advice on what to do and how to do it.

The A to Z format ensures that sections appear under individual headings for instant ease of reference. The emphasis is not so much on the law as on its implications; the advice is expert, clear and practical, with a minimum of legal references. Checklists, procedures and examples are all given as well as warnings on specific pitfalls.

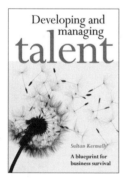

DEVELOPING AND MANAGING TALENT

How to match talent to the role and convert it to a strength

Sultan Kermally

£12.99 paperback, £24.99 hardback

Published May 2004

Effective talent management is crucial to business development and profitability. Talent management is no soft option; on the contrary, it is critical to long-term survival.

This book offers strategies and practical guidance for finding, developing and above all keeping talented individuals. After explaining what developing talent actually means to the organization, he explores the e-dimension and the global dimension. He summarizes what the 'gurus' have to say on the development of leadership talent. Included are valuable case studies drawn from Hilton, Volkswagen, Unilever, Microsoft and others.

HIGH-PERFORMANCE CONSULTING SKILLS
The internal consultant's guide to value-added performance

Mark Thomas
£14.99 paperback, £24.99 hardback
Published November 2003

This book provides a practical understanding of the skills required to become a high-performance internal consultant, whatever ones own area of expertize. It will help you to: market your services and build powerful internal networks; secure greater internal client commitment to initiatives and change projects; enhance your own worth and value to the organization; develop stronger more productive working relationships with internal clients.

EXECUTIVE COACHING
How to choose, use and maximize value for yourself and your team

Stuart McAdam
£12.99 paperback.
Published March 2005

Executive coaching is coaching paid for by an organization to help an individual achieve their full potential at work. This book – by an insider with plenty of experience of hiring coaches and acting as a coach – provides a pragmatic insight into executive coaching for those who:are contemplating a career move and becoming an executive coach; are considering using the executive coaching process for their organization; are considering using – or asking their organization for – an executive coach for themselves.

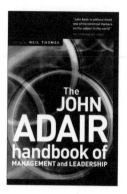

THE JOHN ADAIR HANDBOOK OF MANAGEMENT AND LEADERSHIP

John Adair • Edited by Neil Thomas
£12.99 paperback, £24.99 hardback
Published April 2004

"A book for constant reference ... A great achievement ...ought to be found on every manager's bookshelf."
JOURNAL OF THE INSTITUTE OF PUBLIC SECTOR MANAGEMENT

"... without doubt one of the foremost thinkers on the subject in the world." SIR JOHN HARVEY-JONES

A master-class in managing yourself and others, it combines in one volume all of Adair's thought and writing on leadership, teambuilding, creativity and innovation, problem solving, motivation and communication.

MANAGE TO WIN

Norton Paley
£15.99 paperback, £29.99 hardback
Published February 2005

Learn how to reshape and reposition your company to meet tougher challenges and competitors, when to confront and when to retreat, how to assess risk and opportunity and how to move to seize opportunities and knock-out the competition. Real-life case-studies and examples throughout the text. Extensive appendix of practical guidelines, numerous management tools and usable checklists.

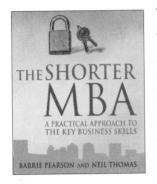

THE SHORTER MBA

A practical approach to the key business skills

Barrie Pearson and Neil Thomas

£35.00 Hardback

Published July 2004

A succinct distillation of the skills that you need to be successful in business. Most people can't afford to give up two years to study for an MBA. This pithy, practical book presents all the essential theory, practice and techniques taught to MBA students – ideal for the busy practising executive. It is divided into three parts:

1. Personal development

2. Management skills

3. Business development

Thorogood also has an extensive range of reports and special briefings which are written specifically for professionals wanting expert information.

For a full listing of all Thorogood publications, or to order any title, please call Thorogood Customer Services on **020 7749 4748** or fax on **020 7729 6110**. Alternatively view our website at **www.thorogood.ws**.

BUSINESS SEMINARS

Focused on developing your potential

Falconbury, the sister company to Thorogood publishing, brings together the leading experts from all areas of management and strategic development to provide you with a comprehensive portfolio of action-centred training and learning.

We understand everything managers and leaders need to be, know and do to succeed in today's commercial environment. Each product addresses a different technical or personal development need that will encourage growth and increase your potential for success.

- Practical public training programmes
- Tailored in-company training
- Coaching
- Mentoring
- Topical business seminars
- Trainer bureau/bank
- Adair Leadership Foundation

The most valuable resource in any organization is its people; it is essential that you invest in the development of your management and leadership skills to ensure your team fulfil their potential. Investment into both personal and professional development has been proven to provide an outstanding ROI through increased productivity in both you and your team. Ultimately leading to a dramatic impact on the bottom line.

With this in mind Falconbury have developed a comprehensive portfolio of training programmes to enable managers of all levels to develop their skills in leadership, communications, finance, people management, change management and all areas vital to achieving success in today's commercial environment.

What Falconbury can offer you?

- Practical applied methodology with a proven results
- Extensive bank of experienced trainers
- Limited attendees to ensure one-to-one guidance
- Up to the minute thinking on management and leadership techniques
- Interactive training
- Balanced mix of theoretical and practical learning
- Learner-centred training
- Excellent cost/quality ratio

Falconbury In-Company Training

Falconbury are aware that a public programme may not be the solution to leadership and management issues arising in your firm. Involving only attendees from your organization and tailoring the programme to focus on the current challenges you face individually and as a business may be more appropriate. With this in mind we have brought together our most motivated and forward thinking trainers to deliver tailored in-company programmes developed specifically around the needs within your organization.

All our trainers have a practical commercial background and highly refined people skills. During the course of the programme they act as facilitator, trainer and mentor, adapting their style to ensure that each individual benefits equally from their knowledge to develop new skills.

Falconbury works with each organization to develop a programme of training that fits your needs.

Mentoring and coaching

Developing and achieving your personal objectives in the workplace is becoming increasingly difficult in today's constantly changing environment. Additionally, as a manager or leader, you are responsible for guiding colleagues towards the realization of their goals. Sometimes it is easy to lose focus on your short and long-term aims.

Falconbury's one-to-one coaching draws out individual potential by raising self-awareness and understanding, facilitating the learning and performance development that creates excellent managers and leaders. It builds renewed self-confidence and a strong sense of 'can-do' competence, contributing significant benefit to the organization. Enabling you to focus your energy on developing your potential and that of your colleagues.

Mentoring involves formulating winning strategies, setting goals, monitoring achievements and motivating the whole team whilst achieving a much improved work life balance.

Falconbury – Business Legal Seminars

Falconbury Business Legal Seminars specializes in the provision of high quality training for legal professionals from both in-house and private practice internationally.

The focus of these events is to provide comprehensive and practical training on current international legal thinking and practice in a clear and informative format.

Event subjects include, drafting commercial agreements, employment law, competition law, intellectual property, managing an in-house legal department and international acquisitions.

For more information on all our services please contact Falconbury on +44 (0) 20 7729 6677 or visit the website at: www.falconbury.co.uk.